ON THE VALUE OF SECRET PLAYS:

"I can give the opposition advance notice of every play we run, and we'll still win."

—*Vince Lombardi*

ON THE MASTERMINDS AND COMPUTERS USED IN THE PLAYER DRAFT:

"When we go twelve rounds, we're hoping to find three or four players and not too many embarrassments. That means we're hoping to get lucky."

—*Al Davis of the Oakland Raiders*

ON THE WELL-KNOWN FRAGILITY AND INEFFECTIVE-NESS OF SCRAMBLING QUARTERBACKS:

Fran Tarkenton and Don Meredith

And so it goes . . . from the playing field to the front office . . . from the locker room to the commentary on living room TV . . . here is everything that pro football insiders know and that they'd just as soon you never found out . . . in the book that bursts the bubble of—

THE PRO FOOTBALL MYSTIQUE

Other Sports Books from SIGNET

If you wish to order these titles,

please see the coupon

in the back of this book.

The Pro Football Mystique

by

Dave Klein

A SIGNET BOOK from
NEW AMERICAN LIBRARY
TIMES MIRROR

Published by
THE NEW AMERICAN LIBRARY
OF CANADA LIMITED

*NAL books are also available at discounts in bulk quantity
for industrial or sales-promotional use. For details, write to
Premium Marketing Division, New American Library, Inc.,
1301 Avenue of the Americas, New York, New York 10019.*

First Signet Printing, November, 1978

1 2 3 4 5 6 7 8 9

 SIGNET TRADEMARK REG. U.S. PAT. OFF. AND FOREIGN COUNTRIES
REGISTERED TRADEMARK — MARCA REGISTRADA
HECHO EN MONTREAL, CANADA

SIGNET, SIGNET CLASSICS, MENTOR, PLUME AND
MERIDIAN BOOKS are published in Canada by The New
American Library of Canada Limited, Scarborough, Ontario

PRINTED IN CANADA
COVER PRINTED IN U.S.A.

For Wells Twombly

*A friend remembered
for his laughter, warmth,
and magnificent irreverence.*

Author's Note

This book was not intended to demean, belittle, or cheapen the sport of football as it is played by professionals. Quite the contrary; I have an unabiding fever for the game. But I have seen the double-talk and double-think that has elevated pro football from a game to an inexact science made far more serious than it should ever be.

Pro football is marvelous fun. It is hoped that it will be allowed to remain so. What I have tried to do is strip away the veneer of complexity and bring the game back to its basic form, a rather simple, easy-to-grasp diversion for people of all ages and inclinations.

And in the doing, I would like to express special thanks to two close friends, Herb Schnall and Mel Bookstein. Their assistance, guidance, and counsel have been, as always, just a notch less valuable than their friendship.

Dave Klein

Contents

1. Face to Face with the Myth

"Is there a difference between coaching college boys in southern California and professionals in Tampa? Sure. Three thousand miles and a lot more money."
—John McKay, 1976

"It's not as complicated as most people make it [pro football]. I think a lot of coaches have a tendency to make the game difficult because they compound situations and try to set a defense for every situation. You can't do that. It's impossible."
—Johnny Unitas, Hall of Fame quarterback.

Did you ever fantasize, when you were a child, about pulling off the Lone Ranger's mask? How many times during those early radio and television segments did we come excruciatingly close to seeing that mask ripped off by Black Bart? But it never happened.

Do you know why?

Because underneath that mask, he was just another white man.

Now we have created a myth out of pro football. But is it really bigger and better, more mysterious, and more complex than what you played at an age when the Lone Ranger was still important? Is it too complicated for Henry Kissinger to fathom?

The answer is no.

There is still time to defeat this monster of our own

creation. All that follows will be our game plan, our playbook, our computer print-out strategy. Our assignment is no easier or more difficult than attempting to defeat the Pittsburgh Steelers' defense. All we need to find are the creases in the zone, the inherent weaknesses in the overall entity. They have used zones and double coverages and rotating pass-off defenses to try to stop us, but we have the ammunition.

We have the ultimate weapon. It is not a multiple offense or a roll-out quarterback or a pass-catching running back. We go right to the heart of the problem. We have The Truth.

Football is played in the United States for the financial benefit of athletes, coaches, team owners, and television networks, to say nothing of the grown men who sell everything from cologne to underwear emblazoned with the name and emblem of the National Football League team of your choice. The game is well into its second century. The boom is well into its third decade.

This game, which is rather a bastard son of lacrosse and rugby, is not conceptually different today in practice and theory from the first game ever played, an event variously placed in Jeannette, Pennsylvania, Duluth, Minnesota, New Brunswick, New Jersey, or Vince Lombardi's backyard in the Sheepshead Bay section of Brooklyn.

There have been changes, of course. The shape of the ball is different. The complexity of the players' uniforms and equipment, even the size of the players, are radically different. But the basics and the form and the vision of the game are still there, untouched and unchanged.

Players and coaches used to be good old country boys or tough old coal-country boys who played and taught because they loved the game. Now they are aristocrats in jockstraps, financial tycoons in cleats and helmets. They are outrageously overpaid, in a time when social workers, policemen, firemen, and teachers are outrageously underpaid. But their game is astonishingly the same.

The game you might see next weekend will be played no differently than it probably was forty years ago. The tools are the same, the goals are the same, and the means of achieving ends are the same.

There is sufficient evidence to credit the invention of the forward pass with the birth of modern professional football. This ranks somewhat on the lower end of the totem pole of miraculous discoveries and merely serves to prove how slow and unimaginative were the coaches of the day, for they were the self-proclaimed tacticians, the dabblers in creativity and originality.

Various among them have been dubbed progenitors of the game. They have become part of our past, heroes of our nation on a level with Lucky Lindy, Daniel Boone, and the guys who perished in a blaze of glory because there was no back door to The Alamo.

But the forward pass? It is a basic, natural instinct of man to throw that which can be grasped in one hand. When Aargh strolled along prehistoric primrose paths in search of food, was he resigned to eating leaves and roots? He was not. Aargh would pick up a rock—it might have been round, oblong, flat, square, or triangular. He would heft it in his hand (nice, comfortable feeling, isn't it?). He would scan the surrounding area until he saw something delectable. Then he would throw his rock. Assuming he had the necessary accuracy, it would land smack alongside the head of some innocent brontosaur, who cooperated by suffering a massive cerebral hemorrhage and dying on the spot.

When Aargh saw the creature tumble, he knew he had a good thing going. Later, when he brought home the bronto bacon and was joyously rewarded by Mrs. Aargh, he was sure of it.

There is a purely visceral delight to be obtained from hurling an object through the air. It doesn't even have to be aimed at anything specific. (Oh, you've seen the Tampa Bay Buccaneers.) It is proof of one's strength and intelligence and cunning. It is verily existential. I throw, therefore I am.

If Aargh had been strolling along those paths last week, and if he had struck down a pigeon in flight, and if a scout had been in the woods, Aargh would have been given a contract, a uniform, eleven million dollars, and would have become a quarterback. It's as simple as that.

Yet it took a millennium from the first beginnings of butchery until Knute Rockne or Amos Alonzo Stagg or Pop Warner or Craig Morton discovered the forward pass. So how smart can coaches be?

Indeed.

If all this strikes you as somewhat irreverent, and smacks of heresy as well, your perceptual skills are to be applauded. It is intended to be irreverent and heretical, for too many men and women in our society have affixed an almost mystical importance to the game of football. It has become more than a game. It has become a cult. A religion. An obsession.

This mystique has always been with us, along with all sorts of other potential disasters. But until the advent of nationally and interminably televised games, it was a malady relegated to a harmless few.

But now? Now, dear Lord, there are millions of mumblers of the holy litany.

The dying man on his final bed: "Son, lean over so that I may whisper to you the secret and meaning of life."

The tearful son dutifully places his ear to the father's lips, for this is his birthright.

The dying man solemnly gasps: "Fly-Left, X-Over, Y-Zig-Out, Thunder-Trap-Nine. On six."

The son is overcome. Immortality is his.

Clearly, we have created a monster.

Now we begin the exorcism. Let the first truth be known: There are only eleven men on a side in this game. Therefore, perhaps as late as twenty-four hours after the first game was played, some coach had undoubtedly worked out all the practical mathematical combinations and computations inherent in various positionings of eleven men.

He may have settled upon two running backs or three running backs. They might have been lined up in an I-formation or a T-formation or an A-formation or a Box-formation. He may have decided on two receivers or three receivers (positions created with the discovery and refinement of that forward pass), and they may have been stationed next to the offensive linemen or split well away from them or off the line into the backfield or various combinations of all of the above.

Generally, the thrower of the forward pass is the quarterback. He can either throw the ball or hand it off to one of his two or three running backs, variously called fullback, halfback, wingback, tailback, slotback, upback, or setback.

The object is to advance the football in a forward direction. Ideally, it is to advance the football in a forward direction so that the end zone will reach the advancer before a tackler does. This is called a touchdown. The team with more touchdowns at the conclusion of the allotted time, typically, is declared the winner of the game.

Defensively, there used to be eight of the eleven men on the line. That was when every offense did nothing else but run the ball. That was before the genius invented the forward pass.

With the pass came adjustments; slowly, of course. The eight men up front dwindled to six, then five, finally four, sometimes only three. Some of those who used to be linemen were told to move back a step or two and stand upright (as is their birthright). Magically, they became backers of the line. Linebackers. They were still there to make tackles, to be sure. But now, on the off-chance that the ball might be thrown, they were in a better position to chase him to whom it might be thrown, or even to bat down the ball in mid-flight.

Doodling with ink and quill produced a three-man line with four linebackers . . . a four-man line with three linebackers . . . a four-man line with three linebackers and four deep men guarding against long passes into the vulnerable areas . . . a three-man line with three linebackers and five deep backs . . . a four-man line with four linebackers and only three deep backs.

Obviously, the possibilities are many. But not endless. There are only eleven men to a side, then as now, and it was quickly and conclusively proved that eleven deep backs simply wouldn't work well against the run. Or the short pass.

It has come full circle. Today's spectacular chrome-plated, star-spangled defenses feature such radical concepts as a fourth linebacker at the cost of a fourth lineman . . . or a fifth deep back at the cost of a third linebacker . . . or a fifth deep back at the cost of a fourth lineman . . . or a sixth deep back with three linemen and two linebackers. Or whatever.

There is nothing new. Only dormant. Would you like a classic example of coaching overthink? Of course you would.

In 1961, the San Francisco 49ers of the NFL scrapped the T-formation offense, the Holy Grail of pro football, and in its place installed a short-punt formation. This was called the Zephyr offense by the head coach, a man of great vision named Red Hickey. (That is not an affliction, it is a name.) Coaches around the league panicked. There was the quarterback, seven yards deep into the backfield, not immediately behind the center with his hands resting on the other's scrotum awaiting the direct handoff, but accepting a short snap that appeared magically from under the center's upraised tushie.

How could the defensive linemen rush the quarterback into a hasty retreat if he were already there? Great concern and distress swept the league. Hickey was so excited about his new concept that he unloaded a somewhat aging quarterback named Yelverton Abraham (mercifully, Y. A.) Tittle, who was not fleet of foot and, therefore, not capable of doing all the running, sprinting out, and passing on the run demanded of him who would operate the Zephyr.

So Hickey suckered the dumb old New York Giants into trading a talented young offensive lineman, a guard named Lou Cordileone, to San Francisco for the unwanted, unnecessary, fading legend—Tittle. Never let it be said that Cordileone was not a realist. When told that he had been traded for one of the most fabled passers of the time, he responded with genuine and stunned incredulity: "Just me? For Y. A. Tittle? Are they nuts?"

Indeed.

In any case, Hickey's Zephyr rolled along, gathering steam and ebullience and new victims each week. The season opened with a victory over Washington, 30-3. Then came Detroit, 49-0. And Los Angeles, 35-0. And Minnesota, 38-0.

The league was in turmoil. The most incisive minds on all the coaching staffs stayed up night after night viewing film and studying scouting reports. And doodling. How to stop the Zephyr? What secrets can be learned? What defense can be created or improvised to unlock the mysteries of the Zephyr?

The Chicago Bears were next up. They gritted their teeth and admitted to being frightened and intimidated. They despaired of retaining even their pride in the face of such a monstrous onslaught. They even trembled a bit for photographers. And then, on a crisp Sunday afternoon, they beat the crap out of the Zephyr offense. The score was 31-0. The Zephyr lay there on the turf of Wrigley Field, smoldering, in ruins. Hickey and his 49ers were destroyed.

Canny old George Halas, who was the founder of the NFL, the owner and coach of the Bears, and probably the father of Aargh, was besieged with questions as to what miracle he had wrought, what solution he had found to decipher the complexities of the Zephyr. "Bullshit," said canny old George Halas, cannily. "I dug out my old playbooks for defense against the single-wing. That's all the damned thing was, a single-wing offense. Why didn't you jackasses see it all along?"

Because they weren't old enough, canny George.

The single-wing had died with the introduction of the forward pass. Remember? There is nothing new. Only things dormant.

By the way, whatever happened to Y. A. Tittle? Did he limp off into retirement, licking his wounds? He did not. He reported to New York and he drove another legend, Charley Conerly, into retirement and he took the Giants to three consecutive championship games in 1961, 1962, and 1963. And he never did anything but operate the T-formation offense. He passed a lot. That's what he got paid to do.

The 49ers finished the 1961 season with a 7-6-1 record. They scrapped the Zephyr offense and went back to the T-formation.

"If we only had a passing quarterback," Hickey moaned at midseason, "we'd be winning more games."

Like Tittle, Red?

"Yeah," he said glumly. "Like Tittle."

Indeed.

Once professional football grew and mushroomed into the many-tentacled monster it is now, the far-thinking coaches and general managers began to investigate the value of computers as a research-and-development aid.

The computer, probably used first by Tom Landry of the Dallas Cowboys, has been relentlessly exploited. Teams fed game plans into it, and it spewed forth counterplans. It became possible to put into the computer the play-by-play history of an opponent's last five years of games, and back came frequencies, trends, and preferences. In other words, let us assume the Michigan Morons had been faced with a third-and-four situation one thousand times. In nine hundred instances the play they called had sent the fullback off right guard. The remaining one hundred opportunities had included sixty sweeps to the right by the halfback, thirty passes to the tight end on the left sideline, and ten more exotic plays, such as a reverse, a halfback option pass, or a quarterback draw.

Moreover, of the 900 fullback-off-right-guard play selections, 850 had resulted in a desired first down. Hence, when faced with a third-and-four, the Michigan Morons were almost certainly going to send their fullback off right guard. The Morons probably didn't even realize this. But it would happen. Tom's transistors practically guaranteed it. So pro football underwent electronic surgery.

Now there was more rigidity, more inflexibility. Now the teams were programmed. Now offenses were told what plays had the best chance of working, and defenses were told the best way, at least theoretically, of stopping the offense. Everybody, of course, did as he was told. Imagination left the offense, and the defense was programmed to counter with equally unimaginative moves. It became a chess game played by amateurs. Move and countermove.

In 1963, I voted for Tom's computer as Coach of the Year. Another computer negated my ballot, which clearly did not compute. Instead of bombs we were given slants designed to gain three yards. Instead of surprises on third-and-one, we were given fullback smashes. Instead of fourth-down drama, we were given punts from the enemy's thirty-five. It might have been logical and correct and proper, but it was dull as hell. Most coaches eschewed the unexpected for what had been proven to work.

Computers began to devise entire game plans. All situations were accounted for . . . all down-and-distance contingencies were plotted and studied. Answers came back from the flashing bulbs, sizzling wires, and electronic print-outs.

—Third-and-seven, they'll pass to the halfback in the left flat 89 percent of the time.

—Second-and-long, it will be sweep left, both guards and the right tackle pulling out.

—Third-and-short, the fullback dives over right guard with the halfback leading the way with a block on the middle linebacker.

—Second-and short, they'll try screen pass left.

Indeed.

The computers were also put to work in the selection of new talent. Warm bodies playing their hearts out for colleges from coast-to-coast became nothing more than coded symbols. Apparently, ideal size requirements were determined by feeding into a computer all the dimensions of all the great players in specific positions. Back came the answers:

—The perfect strongside linebacker will be six three and will weigh 235 and will run the forty-yard dash (pro football's yardstick) in 4.65 seconds.

—The ideal defensive end will be six four and will weigh 260 and must be able to run the forty in 4.85.

—The perfect wide receiver will be six two and will weigh 197 and will run the forty in 4.55, and likes to live alone, is a bit neurotic, and has not yet discovered girls.

And every once in a while the computer would blow one and disintegrate into a flashing of blushing red lights and a clattering of embarrassed bells. For a linebacker would be found sitting forlornly by his telephone long after the college player draft had been concluded. This study in depression was only six one and 216, you see, and he ran the forty no faster than 4.75. He had been rejected.

Rejected.

By a computer.

But motivated by compassion, pity, and a need for warm cannon fodder, some doormat of a team would sign him on as a free agent. Then, being so moved by this show of pity, he would destroy all the computer's selections and turn into a superstar with killer instincts and blood dripping from his teeth. He would be a football player.

Baltimore linebacker Stan White is an all-pro. He was also a seventeenth-round (that was the last one in those days, men) draft choice. "The way they work the draft is this," he said. "First they take all the All-America selections. Then they try to find sleepers like basketball players or track men. Then they finally get around to the real football players, the guys who play with their faces in the mud and break the other guys' bones. My opinion of the draft is that it stinks."

And every time a Stan White surfaces, people fall on their swords in the catacombs of other teams' offices. Dallas, in fact, has a long and glorious history of finding sleepers, free agents unheralded and unknown as college athletes, and turning them into superstars. But wait. Just how smart does that make the Cowboys? Cliff Harris, for instance, is one of the finest free safeties ever to play this game. He was undrafted, signed as a free agent out of Ouachita Baptist College in Arkansas. Drew Pearson, for instance, is an elusive and precise wide receiver, undrafted and signed as a free agent out of Tulsa University. Both have been annual all-pro selections.

But if Tom Landry and the Dallas Cowboys are so damned smart, how did they miss an all-pro free safety and an all-pro wide receiver in the draft? Why would they allow twenty-five other teams to draft through seventeen rounds? Would they not want to claim such gems early, for is that not the reason for conducting a draft in the first place? To find new heroes? The answer is obvious. They didn't know about Cliff Harris and Drew Pearson. They weren't smart, they were lucky. And they didn't know about such free agents or low draft picks as Cornell Green and Pete Gent and Rayfield Wright, either. All turned into all-pros. And Tom Landry was sneakily unfaithful to his loving computer, too, because those people did not meet the computerized size requirements for their positions.

Yet computers have been so totally insinuated into our lives that we must accept. We are billed by them and we send them payment. We are located and categorized and filed away by them. In the twinkling of an eye, all the necessary data about ourselves are available to anyone who needs it. Credit rating . . . medical history . . . family. . . income . . . occupation . . . predilections as to sex and recreation (often the same thing) . . . marital status . . . speeding tickets. It's all there.

We may all be bent, stapled, and spindled, but that hasn't prevented our cards from falling neatly into place. The computers run our world. We are booked into hotels and onto airplanes via computer. We are paid by computerized check-writers. In fact, our indiscretions—come now, have you never done your own income tax return in the privacy of your own home?—are uncovered by computerized snoops.

So, perhaps in partial surrender, it says here that computers haven't ruined pro football. They have made it duller than it should be, more predictable than it could be, less exciting than it would be under other circumstances. But it is the men who have decided to seek computerized help who must be held accountable.

The head coaches. And Lord knows they need all the help they can get.

One head coach, you see, is basically no different from any other. Yet some are lionized and canonized, while others are ostracized and cannibalized. But they all know the same things.

They can all stand in front of a microphone or a press conference or a blackboard and draw all those cute little X's and O's and say all those dark, mysterious words like loop, stunt, bootleg, blind-trap, quick-draw, and the rest.

What they are doing . . . what they have done . . . is to create and insulate their own world, a carefully structured world pieced together out of confusion, diversion, and subterfuge, and replete with secret terms, code words, and baffling doubletalk. They are protecting themselves. And their jobs. You see, no head coach in the business knows any more than any other head coach, and the sum total of what they know can be grasped, if not verbalized, by any high school player.

I'm sorry, guys, the secret is out. It's done. I hope your world hasn't suddenly gone dark. But it's true. Not only isn't there anything new in football, there isn't anything any more complicated about it than the language head coaches have created in order to shield the truth from the public.

Players, broadcasters, scouts, and a sickeningly large number of print-media representatives have entered into this all-consuming, all-encompassing conspiracy. They propagate the proliferation of this secret language. And the fans, those poor boobs who pay the freight for all of this, have been so anxious to be accepted into this exclusive fraternity that they have sat in their stadium seats, for which they paid far too much far too early in the year, and shouted words with incomprehensible meaning.

After all, what normal, intelligent, well-adjusted attorney, for instance, would admit that he'll argue a corporate tax appeal on Friday, prepare a complex brief on an infringement of copyright on Saturday, and then find himself sitting in a stadium on Sunday, screaming: "Watch for Wanda, you moron . . . here comes the screeno, the screeno . . . look at the strong safety, he's not chucking the tight end . . . misdirection, misdirection . . . look out for the Free Frank Flood zone."

Hey, guys. What the hell are you talking about? And do you really want your kids to watch this performance?

I remember a sportswriter, admitting an indiscretion through a Sunday morning hangover, describing his night out: "I picked up this woman . . . had to be fifty . . . and kind of ugly . . . and we got to her apartment and she took off her girdle and sort of exploded . . . and what the hall, I was drunk, but I remember thinking, What if my kids could see me now?"

The language is the only true barrier.

"Do you want to know the most difficult thing there is in pro football, the absolutely most difficult problem?" asks former Dallas guard Blaine Nye, a man who has an IQ of 162 and a master's from Stanford. "It's the terminology. I talk to guys from other teams, and we all know the same plays and formations.

"But one guy has been taught that a certain formation is called Brown and ours might be called Blue. And one guy knows a play as Slant Thirty-four, and we might use the same play, but we calle it Dive Thirty-five. It's all the same shit, with different words.

"My friends who have been traded swear that the

only tough thing about acclimating has been the job of learning all the new terms. When they do, they realize it's all the same, but only the coaches know it."

In the middle of the 1977 season, tight end Bob Tucker was traded from the New York Giants to the Minnesota Vikings, where he celebrated a reunion with quarterback Fran Tarkenton. They had played together in New York for five years.

Tucker had three days of practice and study with the Vikings. Then he found himself in that Sunday's game against Atlanta. Minnesota won, 14-7. Tucker caught the winning touchdown pass, a six-yarder.

It was a third-down play, and just before it began, Tarkenton beckoned to the bench. In came Tucker. In the huddle, Sir Francis rattled off a string of numbers that meant nothing to Tucker. Then he whispered a sweet nothing to his old/new tight end.

"It's the old Power Twenty-seven, Y-Over," he said.

Tucker smiled. It was part of coach Alex Webster's offensive terminology w-a-y back in 1971. So he blocked down, paused for a count of two, then ran from right to left into the end zone. He and Tarkenton's lobbed pass arrived together.

Merlin Olsen, late of the Los Angeles Rams, as fine a defensive tackle as has ever played this game—he was an all-pro selection in each of his fifteen years in the league—smiled and told all.

"I know this has become a highly complicated and technical game," he said, "but for all the numbers and theories and data, it all comes down to execution. If you don't play the game well, you lose. And more important, football is still a game, the same game I played when I was a kid."

And Jim Otis, a frequently successful fullback in St. Louis, puts it even more succinctly: "You know, this is a very simple game. It's just a matter of going where they ain't."

Indeed.

Even the sainted Vince Lombardi, who coached the Green Bay Packers to their championships throughout the 1950s and 1960s, once betrayed all of his fraternity brothers thusly:

It was the eve of the 1961 championship game—Green Bay against the New York Giants—and a young, naive reporter was granted an eleventh-hour audience. "What's your game plan?" he inquired, wide-eyed.

The Great man grunted. (He grunted a great deal, Lombardi, but the image-makers and legend-writers will never admit to it.) "You want my game plan?" he thundered. "I'll do better than that. I'll give you my game plan on paper. I'll tell you when we'll call a specific play. I'll even call a timeout and come up to the press box and diagram it for you. And then you may tell the Giants. And if they can stop the play, they'll win the game. But they won't be able to stop it and there is no way they'll be able to win because we have the better team and not only do I know it but they know it and the rest of it, all the rest of it, is pure bullshit."

The Packers won that game. The score was 37-0. There was about as much subterfuge and gimmickry as is usually found in a karate chop to the neck or a knee to the groin. Game plan, my ass.

Indeed.

And now, dear reader, we are ready to expose it all. We will take the clichés found in pro football and turn them inside out. We will shatter the myths and the illusions. It might be painful, but view it as a cathartic. You'll feel much better when it's over.

2. *You Must Establish the Run*

"Coaches who insist you must run before you can pass are cheating themselves. You must only move the ball, by any means available."
—Allie Sherman, 1962

Fact: The short pass may be substituted for the running play and its success will make it easier to both run and pass long.

I like Allie Sherman. A lot. And I respect him. More than a lot. He taught me about pro football and he sat with me in darkened projection rooms and explained what I was watching on film, and he added a certain amount of humanity to an otherwise cold and strategy-filled world.

And Allie, by admission of almost every man who ever attempted to coach this game, was an offensive savant. Even those who didn't like him—and there were many—never hesitated to praise his pure football talents.

His detractors found him arrogant, pushy, glib, and self-centered. I did not. Perhaps that was because his honesty and intensity overshadowed any minor gratings of personality. And in the sixteen years during which I have been a paid observer of pro football, I've never been exposed to a more creative offensive mind.

In any case, Allie Sherman, after emerging from a

childhood in Brooklyn and stint as a left-handed quarterback for Brooklyn College, became one of the first real experts in the use and refinement of the T-formation offense.

He was drafted by the Philadelphia Eagles—imagine, a five nine, 165 pound, left-handed quarterback being drafted by the Eagles. The head coach, Greasy Neale, quickly discovered two of Sherman's best talents—sitting on the bench and teaching.

He became Neale's unofficial assistant coach, instructing older and wiser veterans in the T-formation. Then he coached for a living, working his way down from Winnipeg of the Canadian League to the New York Giants.

In 1961, after failing to lure Vince Lombardi away from Green Bay, the Giants named Sherman their head coach. It was the finest second-choice since John Alden. Sherman served as head coach through the 1968 season, by which time a combination of unsatisfactory scouting personnel, incredibly bad drafting, and impossibly inferior athletes cut him down. He was fired nine days before the start of the 1969 season, following a perfect six-game exhibition schedule. The Giants had lost 'em all.

Sherman won three consecutive championships in his first three years with the Giants. He manipulated a team that had already peaked. He convinced aging athletes that they were still capable of strenuous exercise. He devised new offenses and he tailored defenses to fit those who had lost a step of speed.

It is an intriguing bit of human nature that these players, who had found it possible to cash three championship checks, turned on Sherman. Perhaps they resented his prodding. Perhaps his personality did grate. But when he began to dismantle the already malfunctioning machine via trade, they rebelled.

Sherman traded away Sam Huff, Rosey Grier, Dick Modzelewski, and Don Chandler. He convinced those such as Kyle Rote, Charley Conerly, Andy Robustelli, and Jimmy Patton to seek retirement as a viable alternative to the waiver lists.

In all of Sherman's coaching career, the game I remember with the most admiration serves also as a perfect example of why "establishing the run" is really poppycock.

It took place on October 10, 1962. It was played in Yankee Stadium against the Detroit Lions, an awesome defensive team that was engaged in a no-holds-barred race with Lombardi's Packers for the championship of the Western Conference in the then two-conference, pre-merger NFL.

The Lions' strength lay in the middle of their defense. Their two tackles were Roger Brown, a 300-pound behemoth, and Alex Karras, a 250-pounder with the speed of a cobra and a personality to match. Their middle linebacker, Joe Schmidt, was a Hall of Famer and the third-best at his position in the history of the game (after Dick Butkus and Chuck Bednarik).

No team had been able to run against this defense. The Lions came into the game with a 4-1 record, marred only by a 10-7 loss to Green Bay. They were to finish at 11-3. (Green Bay would conclude its championship season with a 13-1 record, the only loss coming at the hands of the Lions later in the season.)

The Giants at that point were engaged in a dogfight in the Eastern Conference with Pittsburgh and Cleveland. They were 3-2 that day. They never lost another game that season.

"I had to convince the assistant coaches and Y. A.

Tittle [the quarterback] to go along with what I wanted to do," Sherman related. "Our best weapon was the pass. Tittle was a master. But he was terrified of that rush line, and he was sure that if he dropped back to throw they'd be on him. He said we had to keep them off-balance by running, and then he said nobody had been able to do that, and our runners weren't the best."

So Sherman convinced Tittle, then a veteran of fourteen (often all-pro) seasons, that the pass was exactly what would beat Detroit. But not with the deep, long, breath-stopping bombs he liked.

"I asked him what his ideal gain would be on any first-down play," Sherman continued. "He smiled. 'A touchdown,' he said. But aside from that, he said a first down should gain five to seven yards in order to set up the so-called 'free down' on the second play.

"I told him I'd get him the five- to seven-yard gains, by passing. We set up an entirely different short passing offense, and we double-teamed Brown and Karras with our linemen and our big backs [Alex Webster and Phil King].

"Y. A. wasn't sure about it, or me, until after the first sequence. 'Al . . . dammit . . . it works,' he said on the sideline."

What Sherman had done was to create a quasi-running attack built on the short sideline pass. Tittle faked to either Webster or King, then proceeded to hit the line and become an additional blocker. The second's indecision—tackle the "runner" or rush the passer?—held up Detroit's Brown and Karras. That was all Tittle needed to go to his tight end, Joe Walton, or one of the wide receivers, usually Del Shofner.

The Giants won the game, 17-14. They didn't

bother to run the ball very much. They didn't have to. They passed it instead.

The dogmatic insistence on running before passing—on running to set up passing—can be traced back to when teams ran almost exclusively, passing only as a flighty aside. Coaches resisted the new offense, the forward pass, even after it became clear that this radical weapon was capable of gaining much more yardage much faster.

But there are restaurants that still insist men wear jackets and ties, right? Those who still support the run-before-pass theory, and there are many, explain it in those terms—couched-in-mystery. "If you can run well, if you can wound a defense by running the ball and gaining ground, it will react to this attack by tightening up. The linebackers and defensive backs will come up [nearer the line of scrimmage] to help the front linemen. Then you have the advantage of more room in the various areas into which you send receivers. When a defense tightens up, it's easier to pass."

But if a defense has to "loosen up" to counter a successful passing attack, doesn't that make it easier to run?

In the 1958 championship game between the Giants and the Baltimore Colts—that fabled sudden death overtime thriller—the Colts were faced with the near-impossible task of driving upfield with less than two minutes remaining in order to attempt a game-tying field goal.

They passed their way upfield despite the presence of running backs such as Alan Ameche, Lenny Moore, and L. G. Dupre. And before you retaliate by saying, "It takes too much time to run the ball in that situation," let it be said that quarterback Johnny Unitas did not throw to the sidelines, where his receivers could have stepped out of bounds to stop the clock.

No, he threw to the middle of the field where only incomplete passes can stop the inexorable ticking away of precious seconds. "There really wasn't much choice," Unitas has said. "Passing was what we did best. That was a crucial situation. It would have been stupid to follow the book. We did what we did best."

And the Giants' defense countered in the manner described above. When Unitas continued to complete passes to Raymond Berry, the Giants' middle line-backer, Sam Huff, was forced to leave his area in order to help cornerback Carl Karilivacz. "When Sam did that, we had it made," Unitas smiled. "We simply had Berry continue his pattern to the middle of the field. He caught the ball where Sam should have been playing. If Huff had stayed where he was supposed to be, that drive would never have been able to continue. But they reacted out of panic."

Teams with similarly potent passing capabilities should try to grasp the fact that they can use the pass as their major, basic weapon . . . that they can pass without apology to the gods of football. A too-rare illustration of the pass preceding the run came from Pittsburgh head coach Chuck Noll during the 1976 season. "When we play Cincinnati, we are more concerned with Ken Anderson's passes than with any other facet of their offense. In the last few years, the Bengals have had something less than an excellent running game. So when it gets to be, say, third and three or four, we're half expecting them to throw for the first down."

The fact remains that teams with unusually strong running ability run first to use up the clock, maintain possession—if "we" have the ball, "they" can't score—and to minimize the chance of a turnover—a fumble being less likely, and probably less dangerous than an interception. When the New York Jets turned pro football inside-out in Super Bowl III by upsetting the heavily favored Baltimore Colts, their very first play was a long, sideline pass deep to the right to wide receiver Don Maynard. It was incomplete. But Lord, the havoc it caused.

Joe Namath, you see, was the Jets' quarterback, and there haven't been too many better passers since Aargh learned to hunt for food. "During that week," Namath recalled, "there was some doubt as to Maynard's condition. He had had a pulled hamstring muscle and it was reported that he couldn't run well. Listen, he was my main receiver, and if they were sure he wasn't up to it, they would have killed us.

"So I went for that deep sideline pass, the one we had used so well all season. And it scared the piss out of them. Once they saw Maynard could fly, and once they saw I was ready and willing to use him that way, they had to respect him. That made it easier for us to run. And [Matt] Snell gained 121 yards, after we loosened them up with that pass.

"And do you know something? Maynard wasn't up to par. His leg did hurt, and he put a super effort together just to go down for that first pass. If I had to use him like that all day, he wouldn't have been able to do it. I guess you could say we suckered the Colts. We showed them what they were afraid of seeing, and it changed their mentality."

Simply put, Namath established the threat of the passing game in order to run.

Most coaches, both on their own and through the utilization of computer study, strive for a perfectly balanced offense. If there are to be seventy plays in a game, they'd prefer to see thirty-five runs and thirty-five passes.

Of course, situations will dictate otherwise. The team that falls behind will be forced to pass more frequently in order to catch up. The team that goes ahead will run more often, if the running game is working, in order to kill the clock and control the ball. It is this ball-control theory that convinces head coaches to live by the run.

"We want to keep the ball, because we can't get hurt that way," said Miami head coach Don Shula during the incredible rash of victories which, over the span of six seasons (1970 through 1975), amounted to a record of 75-19-1, three consecutive Super Bowl appearances, two straight championships.

Shula's offense was run-oriented. Indeed, he had learned that when he was an assistant to Weeb Ewbank in Baltimore. The Colts of those days had Alan Ameche at fullback, and Lenny Moore and L. G. Dupre as halfbacks. Later, Baltimore had runners such as Tom Matte, Don McCauley, Norm Bulaich, and Don Nottingham.

In Miami, of course, Shula put together a powerhouse running game centered around fullback Larry Csonka and the alternating halfbacks Jim Kiick and Mercury Morris as well. But the Dolphins did not run in order to pass. They had Bob Griese at quarterback, and one of the greatest of all wide receivers, Paul Warfield, was his favorite target.

"When we were on offense," Shula said, "we'd show them a Warfield fly pattern, or we'd send Paul down on a deep route, cutting across the middle of the field, heading for the end zone. That would loosen everything up, and we'd be able to go back to the running game.

"Sure we controlled the ball. We wanted to. But we were able to do it by either passing or threatening to pass first. Other teams were just as concerned with our passing game as with our running game. It's an ideal situation when that happens." Indeed.

But what happens to the coach who insists on establishing the run when he doesn't have superior runners? If he's smart, he improvises. If he's not smart, he collects unemployment checks. There are several examples to cite.

First, let us assume a weak running game is accompanied by a superior passing game. The coach who wants to establish the run in order to pass is lost. But he can adjust, as did Sherman. More and more, quarterbacks are throwing to their running backs. No one does this better or with greater success than Fran Tarkenton of the Minnesota Vikings.

Casual observers suggest that Tarkenton was able to carry this through because of the presence of halfback Chuck Foreman, one of the truly talented all-around backs in the game. Not so. Tarkenton's offense was designed to free a back anywhere from two to eight yards downfield. Foreman turned such short passes—the players call them "dinks and dunks"—into long, electrifying gains. But an average gain of four yards on such pass plays would guarantee first downs, and most backs are capable of catching a short pass and then falling down.

"There really isn't any way a defense can stop those short passes we use," Tarkenton claimed. "We send enough receivers into the various areas necessary to occupy the defensive backs. And if they aren't honored, I'll throw long to them.

"When you can isolate your running back against one linebacker [he licked his lips here], there is no way that defender can stay with him. Backs are faster and shiftier and quicker. It's a mismatch. What we do is intentionally create mismatches, although I should add that anybody covering Foreman, or trying to cover him, finds himself in a mismatch.

"Anyway, say they cover my two wide receivers and my tight end. Okay. I can't throw to them. But if those three men are covered well, chances are the defense is playing a zone. It's difficult to cover man-to-man on everybody eligible to catch a pass.

"All right. They're in a zone. I am faced with the alternate choices of using a running play, which includes myself as a potential runner, or throwing to the backs. Generally, it's safer to throw to the backs. And it pays off."

Tarkenton added a final note. "It's easier to stop Foreman the runner than Foreman the pass receiver," he said. "If we can't run, we'll pass. By using our runners. And that would go against what most coaches have been taught. But it works. I don't worry about having to prove we can run before trying to pass. Just moving the ball is enough."

Indeed.

Let us now assume that a team fields a weak passing game and a strong running game. This is not enough to insure success. The run, when used as an "exclusive" weapon, can and will be stopped. There are choices that offer solutions to this problem.

There are, basically, only three methods of practicing the running game. You can run outside. You can run inside. You can run up the middle.

The outside running plays are the sweeps or the wide off-tackle plays. The inside running plays are the off-guard slants. The up-the-middle running plays are just what they sound like, a basic charge through the center's position.

However, if the passing game is not a viable factor, defenses can stack up even the best of the running attacks. So a coach can design and implement play-action passes.

Basically, a play-action pass calls for the quarterback to appear to hand the ball off to a running back, then pull it back and straighten up to pass. This accomplishes many things—the defense, especially the middle of the defense, will be "frozen" into momentary inaction. If the fake is executed with sufficient deception, that decoy runner will even be tackled.

And since anticipation plays such a key role in any credible defense, that instinct can be ruthlessly exploited. The defense knows, going into the game, that the fullback, for example, is the prime ingredient in the opposition's attack. It will "key" him, perhaps even to the extent of assigning a player or players to follow him, to be responsible only for him. Thus, the defense will be conditioned to expect that runner to carry the ball.

In the heat of the game, a play that looks for all the world like a handoff to the fullback will be honored and the appropriate reactions will ensue: chase him, catch him, kill him! This enables the quarterback to force the defense into tightening and one unexpected aerial strike against a bunched-up, run-reading defense will hurt badly. Thus the quarterback with a strong running attack and a weak passing attack will be able to use the threat of the run—without actually running —to open up a passing game, which, by itself, would fall short.

Now let us further assume that a team with an outstanding quarterback and an ordinary running attack is further hampered by the absence of outstanding receivers.

The defense will be expecting the run, or passes to the running backs. The quarterback can counter by throwing high-percentage passes, generally those aimed at the sidelines where the receiver can put himself in front of a defender. If he cannot catch the ball, it will go out of bounds. In other words, the receiver or no one will be able to make the reception.

Two or three such "safe" passes will still produce the desired effect. The defense will have to adjust, perhaps double-team those receivers bound for the sidelines. And, in turn, that will make it easier for average running backs to achieve success. Again, it is a case of using the pass to allow the running game to function.

Clearly, then, a team need not establish the run in order to pass. When you hear a coach insist on that, you may write him off as antediluvian (or at least tradition-bound), and you may expect his offense to function poorly.

The basic tenet of a coach should be that a team must be tailored to the skills of its personnel. Those teams that pass more successfully than they run can and should design an offense to take full advantage of this. The opposite, of course, is also true. Those with a superior running attack will (or should) use it to complement the passing game.

But the fact remains that running need not be the first assignment. Sam Huff, one of the most notable of middle linebackers during his career with the New York Giants and Washington Redskins, once offered this opinion:

"Johnny Unitas was the best damned quarterback I ever played against, and he had some of the greatest receivers I ever saw. Sure, they had Alan Ameche at fullback, but once Unitas showed what a master he was, Ameche's running attempts dropped in a hurry. One year he was carrying the ball twenty-five times a game, and the next year he was down to six or seven carries. They made him a blocking back, to give Unitas more time to throw.

"At the same time," Huff continued, "the best running back in the league was Jim Brown in Cleveland. Nobody was surprised when the Browns ran more than they passed. They'd have been damned fools to ignore Brown's talents and insist on throwing. But they threw enough to keep defenses off-balance, and Unitas called just enough running plays to do the same thing. Cleveland, with Brown, could have passed at any time —even before running."

In 1975, the Cincinnati Bengals led all twenty-six NFL teams in passing offense. They ranked first by gaining a total of 3,497 yards through the air, 64 percent of their total offense. Their rushing yardage was a paltry 1,819 yards. That rushing offense was no better than seventeenth in the league. But Cincinnati finished with an 11-3 record and gained a spot in the post-season playoffs. There were few games in which they were able to establish the run before they were able to pass successfully.

In contrast, during the 1975 season the Pittsburgh Steelers finished with a 12-2 record. They were second in the league in rushing offense and only fourteenth in passing. They gained 2,633 yards rushing, only 2,254 yards passing. Yet they won their second straight Super Bowl championship. And they seldom chose to pass, unless their running game—Franco Harris and Rocky Bleier, in the main—was stopped. They did not have to worry about the pass. Their personnel dictated a concentration on the running game. But traditionalists will now argue that the Steelers did, in fact, have to establish their running game to compensate for a less efficient passing attack.

Nonsense. With quarterback Terry Bradshaw and such receivers as Lynn Swann, Frank Lewis and John Stallworth, the Steelers might well have outranked the Bengals in passing offense, if they were forced in that direction. With Harris and Bleier, coach Chuck Noll tailored his offense to match his personnel.

Another inherent danger in believing the "run before pass" theory is the disastrous effect such thinking can have on defensive units. "Yes, we are usually expecting a team to open their offense with the running plays," admitted Rams' former head coach Chuck Knox. "As a result, there are times when a 'radical' game plan [his emphasis on radical] can burn you early. But you have to prepare your defense for what most teams will do. And most teams will run before they get into their passing attack."

In the first round of the 1976 playoffs, the run-conscious Pittsburgh Steelers took on the Baltimore Colts. On the third play of the game, after two running plays had netted just two yards, Bradshaw threw deep to Lewis. The Colts were helpless, as Lewis gathered in the ball at the Colts' thirty-yard line and pranced into the end zone. He had beaten the double-team defense (Jackie Wallace and Lloyd Mumphord) by twenty yards. It resulted in a seventy-six-yard touchdown play, with just 1:39 having elapsed in the game. Baltimore never recovered. The final score was 40-14. "I saw their defense lining up," Bradshaw said, "and it seemed as though they were ignoring the chance of a pass. How could I let such an opportunity get away? It was almost too easy."

"One play can make the difference in a game and in a season," Vince Lombardi was fond of saying. "The maddening thing is that you never know when that play . . . that opportunity . . . will present itself. But the winning team is the one prepared to execute every play as if knowing it will be that play."

Bradshaw's early, surprise pass was that play. But the Colts gave it to him, because they lived by the theory that a team must run before it can pass.

Conversely, they also died by the same theory. The Colts had quickly slipped into a trailing situation and had to scrap their game plan in order to catch up. That seldom works. The team in the lead can afford to take more chances, and often those chances pay off in further scoring opportunities. How different might it have been if the Colts didn't expect the Steelers to run before they started to pass?

3. The Scrambling Quarterback Controversy

"I weigh 190 pounds. Why should I drop back exactly seven yards and stay there? That's just what the defensive linemen want me to do, and they weigh 250 pounds, and more. They say, 'Let's all meet seven yards in the backfield on the quarterback's chest.' I'll be damned if I make it easy for them."
    —Fran Tarkenton, famous scrambler.

"Tarkenton will win some games he should lose, but with his scrambling he'll lose more he should win. A scrambling quarterback just can't be a consistent winner.
    —Norm Van Brocklin, Tarkenton's first NFL coach and Hall of Fame (dropback) quarterback.

"When Tarkenton played for the Vikings, I had to chase him twice a year. Now that he's been traded to the Giants, I figure that adds about five years to my career."
    —Willie Davis, Hall of Fame defensive end, 1967.

Three so-called scrambling quarterbacks—Tarkenton, Terry Bradshaw, and Roger Staubach—took their teams to a total of eight Super Bowl appearances in the first eleven years of this game-to-end-all-games.

Too often, the strategy-makers in pro football become static in their thinking. No other phase of the game serves as a better example than the dropback quarterback versus the running or scrambling quarterback.

One need only remember the earlier days of pro football, when such formations as the single-wing forced the tailback to run. Some of the more successful "scramblers" included Frankie Albert, Sammy Baugh, Cecil Isbell, and Bob Waterfield, and they ran often—in the case of Albert, almost as often as they passed.

But then the NFL geniuses decided that the advent of the T-formation meant the end of the running quarterback. No longer was it necessary or desirable, they felt, to have their passer risk the injuries prevalent in the open field. They therefore shackled passers, bound their feet, and removed their opportunity to run.

They nurtured passers such as Johnny Unitas, Y. A. Tittle, Norm Van Brocklin, Charley Conerly, Bobby Layne, Milt Plum, Sonny Jurgensen, Earl Morrall, and Rudy Bukich.

Don't run. Just pass. Drop back seven yards and wait for the pattern to develop. If it doesn't, eat the ball. If you happen to get blind-sided while waiting, we'll notify the next-of-kin. Quarterbacks didn't have to bother thinking about running. Most of them delighted in this exemption. "The only time I ever run," said Van Brocklin, "is out of fear."

Then came 1961, and in the NFL there suddenly appeared the twin visions of the expansionist Minnesota Vikings and a young quarterback from the University of Georgia named Fran Tarkenton.

When they began to play, the traditionalists gnashed their teeth. This was heresy, sacrilege, arrogance beyond measure. Here was a new team, which should not be capable of winning a game, actually winning games (three, by the end of the season). And here with a crewcut and fuzzy cheeks was a kid from Georgia, the son of a Baptist minister, running around and gaining yards, buying time and scoring touchdowns, and all the while masquerading as a quarterback.

In their very first NFL game, the Vikings played the brutal Chicago Bears. They won, 31-13. The NFL was astounded. As the season wore on, Tarkenton was responsible for a renaissance. He ran. That first year he gained 308 yards and scored five touchdowns. He also completed 157 of 280 passes for 1,997 yards and eighteen touchdowns.

More important, he eluded would-be tacklers. He whirled and danced and flitted out of their grasp. He was a maddening, frustrating wisp in the backfield. The heavier defensive linemen chased, and finally crumpled in fatigue. And he continued to dance. The league was agog. "He can't last," said Vince Lombardi. "Someone will get to him and end his career. You can't let your quarterback take those kind of risks."

It should be noted that it was not until 1977, nearly seventeen full seasons later, that Tarkenton was injured. He suffered a broken ankle when tackled by Cincinnati's Gary Burley, who was five years old when Tarkenton hit the NFL.

Henry Jordan, one of the Packers' all-pro defensive tackles, once used a line that he was to paraphrase later when talking about Chicago halfback Gale Sayers. "I always thought Tarkenton was the league's first black quarterback," he said, "because I never got close enough to tell otherwise."

Tarkenton had come upon a basic, expansion-team fact—the offensive line was not very proficient at protecting its quarterback. And why, he reasoned, be a sitting duck? "I didn't really run, or scramble, if you like, to gain yards. It's easier to gain yards by throwing the ball. I scrambled to gain time, to elude the tacklers, to stay upright until one of my receivers worked himself clear."

Tarkenton never liked the word scramble. "I do only what I have to do to complete the passes I throw," he said. "In college, I was a pretty good runner. So I move around. If I had the world's best line in front of me, I wouldn't have to scramble."

But defensive game plans went into the paper-shredder. Defensive coaches went into rest homes. Defensive superstars, those wondrous plodding hulks, saw a direct correlation between Tarkenton and coronary incidents.

"He'd go back to pass," Henry Jordan said, "and we'd play it the way we always did. We'd rush the passer. But that would leave the middle open, because the linebackers would go back to help out on pass coverage. And then the little bastard would be scooting past me and into the open areas and big, fat guys just aren't designed to catch a quick little runt like that. I'll tell you this, the basic fear when you played Tarkenton was embarrassment.

"Remember? He would just humiliate you, make you look silly, get the crowd to laugh, not just applaud. We hated him.

"And those spinning moves he'd make when he got chased . . . now he was a guy six feet tall, maybe 190, and graceful. And he was spinning, using all that agility, to get away from guys six four, six five, and maybe 250 or better. No fucking way in the world we could catch him. The little son of a bitch just didn't play fair. He didn't stand back there like he should have, like all the quarterbacks did."

And because he didn't, defenses had no way to react

to him. It was as if they suddenly had to contend with another running back, but one who had the advantage of being able to throw, too. It was a weight lifter trying to catch a dancer. No way. No way at all.

Coaches went into paroxysms of panic. They improvised. They created defensive alignments. They employed a "pincers" method, which had defensive ends rushing in programmed lanes to cut Tarkenton off from the outside. Tackles were instructed not to rush headlong into the backfield, but to make Tarkenton come to them. They also held their lanes, which, obviously, slowed down the overall pass rush and put much more pressure on the linebackers. Clearly, this was not the answer.

The inherent flaw in all of these instructions was that they were designed to stop a running quarterback but did nothing to stop or even harass a passer. So when the defenses took away his run, Tarkenton was pleased to stand in the pocket and pass. It was what he had wanted to achieve all along. When he did that too well, the defenses reverted to rushing and chasing, and he resorted to spinning and scrambling, and it started all over again.

It took George Allen, then the defensive coach of the Chicago Bears and later the head coach of Los Angeles and Washington, to see the forest despite the presence of all those tall, leafy things. "Tarkenton cannot beat you by running," he said. "It is especially difficult for him to beat you by running if you have a lead. He isn't a game-breaking runner, he is an unpredictable passer. If he wants to run, let him. Do not let him pass, and especially do not let him pass on the run. [Linebackers and defensive backs] do not leave your man to chase him [until he crosses the line of scrimmage] because he will pass to the man you left open. Let him run. Do not let him pass. He can't beat you that way."

It was the same theory employed in the National Basketball Association when Wilt Chamberlain was scoring points in batches of fifty, sixty, and seventy a night. After three or four years of some of the most inane defensive schemes ever allowed to escape M*A*S*H 4077, it took Red Auerbach of the Boston Celtics to deliver the message. "Let Wilt score," he said. "Stop the other four guys."

While Tarkenton captured the spotlight and the attention of the fans for his scrambling, he was by no means the only running quarterback. Don Meredith, for instance, broke in with the then-new Dallas Cowboys and did a great deal of scrambling. In his case, as in Tarkenton's, it was out of necessity. Expansion-team offensive lines did not protect quarterbacks very well. But unlike Tarkenton, Meredith ran more to gain yards than to buy time. In each case, it was running out of fear.

"I used to alternate plays with Eddie LeBaron," Meredith recalled. "He'd come in, and if it was a pass he'd try to stand back there and pass. It didn't often work. Why do you think LeBaron is so short? He started out tall, but he got driven into the ground so many times he compacted. Then I'd come in and the play might be a pass. So I'd go back. Hell, I wasn't really interested in running . . . too many gigantic folks roam around in the secondary looking for a little guy they can knock around.

"But if my pass receivers weren't open, and if I heard the hoofbeats and snorts getting too close, I'd take off. Listen, I ran a lot in college and it worked. There was no way I was going to stand back there and get snapped in half. At those moments, the only advantage I had over the monsters was my agility. I used it."

Often, Meredith used it to the displeasure of head coach Tom Landry, the only coach the Cowboys have ever known. Landry, a purist, does not like his quarterbacks to run. But he sensed an advantage in having a running quarterback as compared to a crippled quarterback, so he has at least condoned such antics.

"Sometimes, we were so ragged that when I'd come in with a pass play the guys on the line wanted to know which way I was going to run," Meredith joked. "I think they knew they weren't terrific at protecting the quarterback."

Meredith was a unique character who daily tested the patience and sense of humor of the methodical Landry.

"I remember in our first year or two," Meredith said, "in a game against the Giants . . . they were great then, especially their defense. Anyway, I call a play in the huddle and we get to the line of scrimmage and I start to call the signals, and then I just plain forgot. I was right in the middle of a call, and my mind went blank.

"It was something like four . . . sixteen . . . twenty-seven . . . uh . . . uh . . . uh . . . AW SHIT! And the Giant defense started laughing like banshees and one of the linemen fell over the line of scrimmage and we got five yards for offsides. From then on, the guys referred to my AW SHIT! play. Even Tom smiled. I think."

So Tarkenton and Meredith began to run, albeit for different reasons, and when it worked, several other teams started looking for their own mobile quarterbacks. Suddenly scouting reports on college quarterbacks included such phrases as "runs well" . . . "has good agility" . . . "has a feel for broken field" . . . "can get out of trouble" . . . "can escape a heavy rush." It had turned again, and eventually the trend produced players such as Greg Landry of Detroit, Archie Manning of New Orleans, Steve Grogan of New England, Bert Jones of Baltimore, Ken Anderson of Cincinnati, Mike Livingston of Kansas City, Joe Theismann of Washington, Richard Todd of New York, Pat Haden and James Harris of Los Angeles, and Jim Zorn of Seattle.

All of them can pass with professional accuracy, but all of them are dangerous when they take off and run, too. And that places significant stress on the defensive teams.

In 1976, Grogan scored twelve touchdowns by rushing. He also gained 397 yards on the ground, and yet found time to complete 145 of 302 passes for 1,903 yards and eighteen touchdowns. The Patriots played to an 11-3 record.

In 1972, Bob Douglass of the Bears accomplished what few running backs ever achieve—he gained 968 yards by rushing, and twice had four-touchdown games.

The 1976 quarterback rushing-and-scoring figures show that almost 10 percent of the league's rushing yardage and more than 10 percent of the league's rushing touchdowns were accounted for by quarterbacks.

What does all this prove?

Among other things, it becomes clear that the game has changed at its most basic level. The quarterbacks no longer stand in the pocket waiting to either complete a pass or be hit. The offensive playbooks are beginning to show plays designed specifically for the quarterback—running plays. The colleges that use the

Veer offense, in which the quarterback runs more than he passes, are being studied much more intensely.

Chuck Fairbanks, who adopted the Veer while head coach at the University of Oklahoma and earned national championships there, still considers such plays intriguing for the NFL teams. "You can't use the Veer in the pros, not as a fulltime offense. But for an occasional play to surprise the defense, I can't think of anything better."

There is still a marked difference between the quarterback who scrambles (Tarkenton) and the quarterback who runs to gain yards (Grogan). The latter is not considered a scrambler. But players like Grogan, scouted as mobile athletes, have the ability to scramble. And it is this trend that has been chiefly responsible for the change in defensive linemen in the last decade or so, for they are now quicker, faster, and perhaps lighter. Greater emphasis has been placed on pursuit because of the mobility of this new breed of quarterback. And so, the NFL appears to be pleased with its collection of running or scrambling quarterbacks.

One wonders how many remember conversations such as the following:

COACH: "You'll never win with a running quarterback."

FAN: "Really, coach? Why?"

Coach can then go into, like, hours of gobblydegook about scrambling and running, and say things like "stationary vision" and "passing planes" and things like that, and the fan goes home with his head spinning and his chest expanded. He knows football now, right?

But now the coach has a different tune to play.

COACH: "In today's game, you must have fluidity in your backfield."

FAN: "Huh?"

Coach can then do his new number. "Well, with the increasing size and speed of the defensive players, and the problem of those giants obscuring vision when you're standing still, we need rolling passes and sprint-out passes and floating pockets and . . . well, see?"

FAN: "Yeah, coach. Boy, isn't that something!"

So when Van Brocklin put Tarkenton down, it had nothing to do with football. It was personalities and attitudes, and a very strong resistance on Van Brocklin's part against learning a phony new language. It was cuter, see, to ridicule the scrambler, because since Van Brocklin's legs had been bound, he didn't have the scrambling experience in his head.

But he did have a reputation for being a funny guy, so he knocked Tarkenton and made fans laugh. It was quite another thing, of course, to stop Tarkenton's scrambling when they moved on to different teams. Then Van Brocklin's defenses made the fans laugh.

But we are with the scrambler/runner today, only the coaches don't call it that anymore. It's mobility. Or fluidity. Or the roll-out alternative. Or the sprint-out potential.

The name of the game remains the same: Move The Ball. If it is ever conclusively proved to the majority of coaches that the ball can best be moved by giving it to the left tackle, then we will enter into the Age of the Tackle . . . the Tailback Tackle . . . the Tackle in Motion . . . the Tackle-oriented Offense. It would be just something else with which the coaches could create a new mystique. The identity and specifics of the current mystique are secondary to the existence of a mystique, any mystique.

In point of fact, the running quarterback brings with him far more excitement and drama than the stationary quarterback. After all, isn't it nicer, instead of watching the passer drop back, frantically search for a receiver, skip around while his blocking crumbles and his protection disintegrates, and then, so a drooling linebacker shouldn't hurt him too badly, fall to the ground, to see the quarterback become a runner, give the drooling linebacker a little hip fake, an eye feint, a shrug of the shoulder, and then sprint off into No Man's Land?

Sure it is. There he goes, into the land of the Mean Men, each one of them panting for the chance to tear off his arms, into the face of incredible danger and risk, and as he continues to advance and danger increases, the crowd is on its feet, cheering. The quarterback can buy time if he scrambles; he can capture the crowd and demoralize the defenses, if he scrambles and runs.

I love running quarterbacks. But I'm not a defenseman. I want my quarterbacks to run. I want to see him turn the gigantic hulks into tottering, teetering titans, out of breath, collapsing, falling all around him, while this vision of athletic excellence flits and phantoms his way deep into enemy territory, daring the odds and the linebackers and getting gorgeous, improvised assistance from his teammates, who suddenly materialize from nowhere to drop a tackle or a free safety with a crunching, soul-satisfying block.

How many times does the skinny little wide receiver get a chance to sneak up on Mister Mean and knock him on his ass? It's beauty, man! It's poetry, and if Y. A. couldn't run, tough Tittle. Now I know what I missed during my younger years. I missed running quarterbacks. (I also missed on IBM and Xerox, but this is a football book, not *True Confessions*.)

What does the running quarterback do for his team? He injects added potential, basically. In effect, he says:

"Hey, guys, if you can't get clear, or if you other guys can't hold your blocks, don't worry. I'll get away and we'll still get the yards, and if I can I'll run out of bounds, and if I can't I'll go as far as I can and then I'll fall down and curl into that fetal position and let the slobs fall on me. It won't hurt."

He loves it, too, you see. It's action. And it's retaliation.

"I used to have nightmares," said Bobby Layne, "about not seeing the crazed water buffalo coming at me from behind, and just as I see my receiver break into the open I get stuck in the back by 260 pounds of fury and six hours later I wake up dead."

But Layne couldn't run, you see, or wasn't allowed to, so his nightmares were usually impossible to stop. Did Tarkenton have the same nightmares? Sure he did. But he solved them. He ran away from the terror, and suddenly he caused nightmares for the gargantuan linemen, too—nightmares of falling down or tripping on their size-fifteen shoes or being laughed at by sixty thousand people.

Sammy Baugh used to be able to handle his nightmares. He played in the days when face bars were a sign of sissiness, and when a defensive player got through once too often, or delivered a particularly stinging blow (especially a late one). Sammy would instruct the appropriate offensive lineman to miss his block.

The lineman would smile, because he knew what was coming. And the play would start, and here would come Godzilla, proud of himself for having beaten the block, arms high to obscure Baugh's vision, eyes shining with the thought of new blood on his talons, a new head for his rear-view mirror. And Baugh would throw the ball. As hard as he could. Into the face of Godzilla.

Those who recovered trod cautiously forever more. Baugh justified this practice thus: "I can't get my shots at them, but they can tee off against me like I was a punching bag. I want them to remember."

There is, of course, a danger in the selection of your running quarterback. By definition, he must also be able to pass with a reasonable amount of proficiency. That, indeed, is the key; the implied threat to pass while running, or to run after pretending to pass, is what keeps defenses bamboozled.

Finally, there isn't anything very new in the double threat of a man who can run and pass. You older folks will remember them as option-halfbacks, and perhaps the finest practitioner of this maneuver was Frank Gifford.

Frank was a magnificent football player, one who spent his entire career with the New York Giants and was rewarded with a place in the Pro Football Hall of Fame, a sort of doubleheader for him since he is already installed in the College Football Hall of Fame. (That he will probably never make it into the Broadcasters' Hall of Fame shouldn't distress him greatly. What the hell. Two out of three ain't bad.)

Gifford did some quarterbacking—and/or tailbacking—at the University of Southern California, where the Giants made him a first-round draft choice in 1950. When he began to make his way in the NFL, he became a master of the double-option, pass or run. Someone decided to draw up more plays for him in which he was given that choice. Hence, more option plays. Frank would take a pitchout handoff from the quarterback (usually his running mate at Toots Shor's, Charley Conerly) and break for the sidelines, brandishing the ball over his shoulder and making several pumping motions as if to throw it.

That sometimes caused the pursuers to brake sharply and leap, at which point Flawless Frank would tuck it under his arm and run. If, on the other hand, the defenders disbelieved Gifford's ability to pass, he would do just that. He became one of the NFL's most feared offensive threats, a man against whom game plans were devised.

Frank was (is) also devilishly handsome, which made him a triple-threat, one would imagine. And the offensive coach of the Giants in those days, Vince Lombardi, was so enamored of Gifford's abilities, if not his looks, that he searched for a latter-day Frank when he took over as the Dictator of Green Bay.

He found one. Paul Hornung.

Hornung had even more potential than Gifford. He could run, pass, placekick, and claim Notre Dame as his alma mater. He was also devilishly handsome, though much more Aryan in appearance (and more prone to surplus poundage) than Gifford. Reports insist that the variation in looks never got in either's way.

It should have come as no surprise, then, when folks such as Tarkenton, Meredith, Landry (Greg), and Douglass appeared on the scene. But trends in pro football tend to be resisted, and these running, scrambling quarterbacks presented a radically new approach to the game. The old coaches had to chew on it for a while.

"It's just college bullshit," said Lombardi, who had things just the way he wanted them with Bart Starr at quarterback. "You can't ask your quarterback to run. Someone will kill him."

Wrong. What happened was that defenses were forced to change and concepts had to be reviewed and altered. Tarkenton was mostly responsible, although his scrambling never approached the yardage totals

reeled off by such as Landry. But his flair and style—
and results—were unmistakable. Tarkenton changed
the game and what you see and hear now is the
consequence: Coaches want running quarterbacks. One
suspects that even Van Brocklin, who now raises
pecans instead of players, would go along with the new
thinking. It is, after all, trendy.

There is, of course, another side to this question. Do
we need a running quarterback to win, or can we win
with the classic drop-back, protect-me quarterback?
The answer, as it is to most everything else in pro football, involves the quality and limitations of personnel.
If a team has a sound offensive line to protect the
quarterback, solid running backs to achieve a run-pass
balance, and fleet and deceptive receivers, the quarterback can stand in the pocket for as long as it takes his
pattern to develop and his target to clear.

If the personnel is there.

Let us study the Oakland Raiders and their ace
quarterback, Ken Stabler. He ran only seven times in
1976 and gained a total of minus-two yards. Stabler
does not like to run. But he also won thirteen of fourteen regular season games, one playoff game, one
conference championship game, and one Super Bowl.

Clearly, he did not have to run in order to win. He
also won the league's passing championship with a rat-
ing-point total of 103.7. It should be added that only
the NFL can explain its formula of rating quarterbacks
as passers, but in an effort to simplify and clarify such
things for us mortals, there is a thirty-six-page
pamphlet available, crammed full of such goodies as
conversion charts, tables for point allocation, and a
synopsis of what the system means, which might be
more understandable if it were written in Sanskrit.

In any case, we are led to believe that Stabler's score

of 103.7 was sensational. That becomes clear—or un-
clear—when the NFL next informs us that, while the
scoring system is based on a nice, round number like
100.000, it is not the best possible score attainable.

Got that?

But we digress. Stabler obviously had no need to
run. There were five primary reasons for this. Their
names were Art Shell, John Vella, Gene Upshaw,
George Buehler, and Dave Dalby. They were the starting offensive linemen of the Oakland Raiders. Two of
them—Shell and Upshaw—are perennial all-pro
selections. The other three either should have been,
have been already, or will be. Soon.

There is a sixth reason, with the unlikely name of
Mark van Eeghen, from the unlikely college of Col-
gate. He is a 230-pound fullback who blocks with
all the fury of a starving sumo wrestler, and he's nice
to have around just in case a blitzing linebacker should
suddenly appear on the scene lusting for Stabler's
body. But Stabler never had to run. Not ever. His
greatest danger while waiting in the Oakland pocket
was terminal boredom.

We can swerve into all sorts of theories and sub-the-
ories involved in this run-or-not question. In the days
of the "classic" dropback quarterback, most teams
placed heavy emphasis on quality offensive lines. But
at the same time, defensive players were more human-
sized. As the defensive linemen and linebackers got
larger, it became more of a problem to contain them.
So the classic dropback passer found himself, with
greater frequency, on his classic dropback ass.

He began to run. The offensive linemen became
more agile—more correctly, more agile offensive linemen were found—and thus they protected the running

quarterback from the equally more agile defensive linemen while everybody, it seemed, was on the run.

Now the quarterbacks *must* run or perish; unless they play for Oakland or St. Louis or one of the other teams with nearly invincible interior lines.

In Super Bowl IV—Kansas City against Minnesota—the Chiefs unveiled what head coach Hank Stram liked to call "The Offense of the Seventies." It featured a great deal of variety and trick plays, but mostly it offered quarterback Len Dawson, old even then, existing in what Stram called a "floating pocket" of pass protection.

That was the key to the offense. At the snap of the ball, Dawson would drop back. But not straight back. He might sprint seven yards to the north-northwest. Or seven yards to the north-northeast. In any case, at an oblique angle to the line of scrimmage. And so would his protectors. And as if by magic, a pass pocket would form wherever Dawson went.

The opposing players, especially the Vikings, were confused by all this. Stram and Dawson and the Chiefs had them flustered. No longer could such assassins as Alan Page and Carl Eller make their usual charge into the backfield to hunt down the quarterback. No longer could they use their speed and quickness to beat the offensive linemen. Now they had to suddenly move laterally, and that gave not one but two or three linemen a shot at them before they could inflict significant damage to the pocket or, even better, to Dawson. As a result, the Vikings were demolished in Super Bowl IV. (The NFL chooses to affix roman numerals to its Super Bowls, but you may feel free to say things like "the fourth Super Bowl" if you wish.)

Stram exulted, as only a short, round man who wears red vests can exult. Bud Grant (the Vikings' coach) went home to study, which is probably the only pastime left to those who spend their winters in Minnesota. It might be noted that as the head coach, Grant had a vested interest in his homework. What he resented most was the embarrassment. This attitude is not to be confused with the German who, upon losing the World Chess Championship to a Russian in 1933, stood, bowed formally, and said: "It is not the championship I regret losing. It is the prize money."

Grant's regret was not the prize money. It was the loss of face, since his defense had been established as the finest in all of pro football. He studied all winter in frigid Minnesota, where the only alternative seems to be fantasizing about being burned at the stake. (Anything ... do it ... just make me feel warm again.)

Happily, the schedule-makers cooperated. The Chiefs and the Vikings were paired in the season opener for 1970. The score was 27-10. The Chiefs had 10. "So much," intoned a vengeful Grant, "for the 'Offense of the Seventies.' We beat it with the 'Defense of the Sixties.' "

What had happened? How did the Vikings, so mortified in January, recapture their glory in September? Was it an exotic philosophy, an extrasensory vision? Did Grant dabble in the occult or make a deal for his soul in return for retribution?

Nah. He played a gap defense. He stretched his defensive line. He opened it up. And what did this do? It enabled Eller and Page and the others to make better use of their quickness. In effect, it cut off the Kansas City offensive linemen before they could sprint away and set up the floating pocket.

Dawson's pocket fell apart quickly. Finally he went back to the classic dropback style . . . seven yards deep, set up, plant the back foot, look for the receiver

. . . get knocked on your ass. Page and Eller and, mostly, Grant, had extracted their revenge. And it was the end of the "Offense of the Seventies."

Stram subsequently left the Chiefs and a few years later was given money equivalent to the Bolivian national budget to become the head coach in New Orleans, a team that had never enjoyed a winning season despite John Mecom's endless wealth.

At last report, the Saints still were looking for that elusive winning season. But their roster was starting to fill up with tremendously large folks. Perhaps Henry was preparing the "Elephants of the Eighties."

The final answer to whether the quarterback should run or remain stationary is, apparently, this: If he can run, by all means let him. If he can't, protect him well or find someone who can, and it that doesn't work, find a quarterback who can run.

4. The 800-Pound Gorilla

"I'm gonna put my kid on steroids, so he can build up extra muscle and make it to the pros."
—Too many fathers

"I don't have much regard for fans. They can yell and scream and boo and throw things. Who cares? They don't have the foggiest damned idea of what's happening on the field anyway. Screw the fans."
—Craig Morton, Pro Quarterback

"Can you imagine? I waited outside the stadium for two hours so my kid could ask that yo-yo for his autograph. Then the yo-yo walks out and shoves my kid aside. Who the hell does he think he is?"
—Too many fathers.

"Almost every player in the NFL went to college. Lots of them even have degrees. I have a feeling they all majored in Showering After the Game, and the ones who don't have degrees flunked the course."
—Unidentified Sportswriter

Q: Where does an eight-hundred-pound gorilla sit?
A: Anywhere he wants.
—Tired Old Joke.

Size is the first step in the creation of awe. Pro football players are big, far bigger than real people, and this is of great importance to fans. They want their heroes to be larger-than-life. Pro football meets that requirement, as does pro basketball. Baseball and hockey players don't make it. They aren't heroically large, just simply well-developed. They don't inspire awe, but they are much more accessible to the fan, so they inspire respect. And identification.

Size has become a blind spot. The coaches are so intrigued with bigness that normal-sized athletes don't get a real chance, despite their potential abilities. In the summer of 1975, the NFL Players Association called a strike, and the veterans, by and large, stayed away from training camp. Given all that time with a collection of draft choices and free agents, the coaches discovered that some of them could actually play the game. As a result, there were more rookies on 1975 rosters than ever before.

(When the resultant domino theory pushed large numbers of veterans back into civilian life, they didn't think the strike was nearly as good an idea as it had sounded in July.)

"We just don't think he's big enough to play tackle," a coach will say about a hopeful prospect. "After all, he's only six-two and 220. Maybe he can be a linebacker, if he has enough quickness."

Try to imagine a guy six-two and 220. Okay? Now try to imagine him as being too small, too light, too short. Does he sound fragile? Puny? Anemic? According to the United States Bureau of the Census, the average American male in the year 1970 stood five eight and tipped the balance bar at 147. And here we have an unfortunate young man who is too short at six two and too light at 220. (Aside: In the NBA, Nate Archibald's nickname is "Tiny" because he is only six one.)

Or how about this, said about Richard Wood, an All-America linebacker at the University of Southern California, when he was drafted by the New York Jets: "If we can get some meat on his bones, build him up some, we might have something here." Poor Richard Wood. He was only six two and he didn't weigh an ounce more than 220.

The size of pro football players today has had an anesthetizing effect on the fan. One simply grows numb from studying rosters. It seems that every player is six one and weighs at least 200 pounds. And those who do come in "just under the wire" are referred to as scrawny.

The danger is total acceptance. By spending too many hours with a pro football team, the athletes begin to don the cloak of normalcy. Isn't everybody the same size? Hey, after all, there's a little cornerback over there and just look at him standing next to that defensive end. He's really little, man. What the hell, he's only six one and 190.

Six one and 190! He is five inches and forty-three pounds above the national average for the American male. What this has done is remove the dream of equality from the fan. Most of you remember the boyhood fantasies; you pictured yourself pulling on a uniform and strapping on the shoulder pads and then catching the winning touchdown pass or tearing through the offensive line or blind-siding the quarterback. Didn't you? Or perhaps you envisioned yourself hitting the home run into the centerfield seats. Or grabbing the rebound and going up for the winning basket with one second left in the game. Remember?

Today, unless you are six four and 240, you simply cannot sustain such daydreams about football. A shadowy area has grown up between the field and the fan. Now pro football has become entertainment and fiction, and altogether unattainable. The vital human connection has disappeared. Now we stare at the athlete, ponder his accomplishments, and wonder at his size. But without hope of ever becoming part of the dream.

How can we relate to Mean Joe Greene of the Steelers? Mean Joe is six-four and 275, he eats Oldsmobiles, lifts trees out of the ground, and bench-presses houses. Ed "Too Tall" Jones of the Cowboys is six nine and weighs 280 and spends his free time swatting birds out of the air.

How can we Walter Mitty ourselves into a ruthless, relentless linebacker, swiftly cover improbable acres of ground, arrive just in time to slap aside the 250 pound guard and grab the 220 pound fullback and pick him up and slam him to the rock-hard Astroturf? We have lost touch with pro football's human connection. For good. Now we can only gaze in wonder. We can no longer identify. It is a loss to be mourned in the dreamworld of sports, which has long kept grown men from thinking as grown men, which has encouraged grown men to think as small boys. But what are the pro football trend-setters left with? Size, baby, but not always talent.

In 1962, the Green Bay Packers drafted Dave Robinson, a defensive end, from Penn State. They made him a linebacker. He was six four and 240. He was a star. From then on, every team had its Dave Robinson standards to fill. But how many people at six four and 240 can play linebacker? Few. Damn few. Which is why Dave Robinson was a star.

When the Giants drafted defensive end Larry Jacobson from the University of Nebraska, they said that the two-time All-America from the national champion

Cornhuskers was six six and 260. Then they said, "He has to work on his upper-body strength." At six six and 260, especially on the first round, one might assume he was already equipped with upper-body strength.

He never made it. He was big, but not strong. He was big, but not quick. He was nearly half a foot taller than his teammate at tackle, John Mendenhall. John has been an all-pro. But surely, at six one, John was simply too small to play the defensive line, wasn't he?

He was not. Jacobson was big. But not very good.

Size, then, is only one way that the pro football player has been elevated beyond the fans' identification with him. It is the most visible difference, but by no means the most vital. Which brings us to money.

There are at least two points of view concerning the amount of money and fringe benefits bestowed upon the NFL player. One point of view belongs to the players. The other belongs to all those who are not players.

In the interests of fairness, let us begin with the players, and let us state that they have much validity on their side. There is no less reason to pay O. J. Simpson $450,000 per season than there is to offer Buddy Hackett $75,000 per week in Las Vegas. Both are in the entertainment business. On the other hand, there is no real reason either of them should earn that sort of money, that is, if we base it on what the average fan earns. But that is an enormous IF. Accurately, we cannot compare O. J.'s yearly salary, or Buddy's weekly salary, with that of the corner candy store owner, the neighborhood insurance salesman, or the local appliance repairman.

They are not in entertainment. Athletes are. And the critical difference is that no one will buy a ticket to watch your Uncle Albert sell shoes or to see how your friend Murray fixes a garbage disposal. But they will pay to see O. J. run . . . to hear Buddy Hackett's endearing obscenities.

If fairness were all that mattered, would it be possible to pay entertainers or athletes more money than policemen or firemen, teachers or social workers? Of course not. To do so, under the laws of logic alone, would be to dabble in absurdities. The impact made on society by an entertainer cannot begin to approach the impact registered by the police, or social workers, or doctors who run ghetto clinics, or teachers who mold and shape and find paying their bills nearly impossible.

But society creates its own aristocrats, if for nothing more noble than to provide an escape, a diversion. The cop and the teacher need something to do. Many of them enjoy a football game. So they buy a ticket and attend. It is, in a very real sense, a hobby, much the same as coin collecting or fishing and boating.

But fish do not have to be paid, athletes do. And so they are paid, and it is to their credit that they have come to demand the last nickel available to them. For their service is not in the scoring of touchdowns or in the blocking of opponents, but in the entertainment they provide for the fan in the stands who has paid his way into the stadium and, as a result, has contributed his fraction toward paying these entertainers in cleats.

In truth, we pay for all our diversions, whether it be through the purchase of a ticket, the time we spend tolerating television commercials, the state taxes needed to stock rivers and lakes, and the admission charged at beaches or to movie theaters.

So be it.

The players earn big dollars. Fine. For just as long as the fans will buy tickets and stare at the tube, the networks will pay the teams bigger dollars for the right to televise games. And the networks, all of them profit-hungry organizations, will then earn back that outlay plus a considerable profit by selling sponsors advertising time during the games. The sponsors are eager to be charged for the time, for they know the fans at home will be watching and, as a result, absorbing the messages that extol the virtues of deodorants, razor blades, and automobiles.

Besides, advertising dollars are deductible, generally falling under the heading of promotion and development expenses. So if the fans stopped coming or watching, networks would stop televising, sponsors would stop footing the bill, and suddenly football players would be on their own, so to speak, in their earning a living.

Most NFL players have been to college. Several have even graduated. A few actually majored in subjects that required a great deal of intelligence and concentration. But most, given their qualitative education, would not have an easy time finding well-paying work. If lawyers and accountants are having difficulty in the current job market, not to mention all the poor souls who majored in elementary education or, God forbid, liberal arts, a physical education major with a minor in deodorant application might have some problems earning in excess of $10,000 annually.

It is, directly or indirectly, the fan who pays the player, who in turn provides the escape, the diversion, and the enjoyment for the fan. Too many players feel, as countless superstars have expressed, little or no regard for the fan. "What do they know about football? They just show up, eat and get drunk, and yell and scream, so how can they be 'experts' in the game we play?"

These stars miss the point, which is twofold: Fans aren't experts and they don't have to be. The folks who cheered when Neil Armstrong set foot on the moon didn't have the foggiest notion of aerospace technology or any of the other mind-bending persuasions that had to be mastered to put Armstrong up there in the first place. But they cheered. They were, in a very real sense, fans.

And they cheered for the same reasons they cheer for a touchdown pass, a sixty-yard run, a quarterback sack, or an electrifying interception. They don't have to know why or how it happened. They are pleased to simply see it happen and to thus feel a part of it.

Players don't understand this, nor will they readily admit that Armstrong on the moon was much more important and dramatic than Namath-to-Caster or Stabler-to-Biletnikoff. Their job, their life, their passions, naturally, rank among their most important activities. The problem is in priorities.

"When I get out in public," said Alex Webster, who was a high school All-America, a college All-America, an NFL and Canadian League All-Star, and a head coach, "people still remember me, especially around New York, where I was born and where I live. Sometimes, like at a hockey game, they stand up and cheer me. It's damned embarrassing. But look, I am so damned grateful for everything that football did for me that I try hard to return it. If a guy wants an autograph and if he says it's for his son, I know damned well it's probably for him. But so what? I'll ask his son's name and I'll write a little message and he's happy. And you know something? It makes me feel good, too. It's an honor."

That is one view. It is a minority view.

Most of the acknowledged superstars tend to shy

away from public appearances. The aristocrat seldom mixes with the peasants. The demands—autographs, answers to questions, requests to pose with someone for a photograph—are annoying.

"Lots of people seem insulted when I tell them I need a fee for appearing at a dinner or a function as a speaker," said former all-pro running back Ron Johnson, an intelligent, articulate graduate of the University of Michigan and a number one draft choice of the Cleveland Browns. "Then they say, 'Well, okay, how about a hundred bucks?' and I refuse. When I tell them what my fee is, they get angry and say things like 'ungrateful' and storm off. The thing is, they don't understand our position."

There is truth in this. Fans don't understand the players' economic position. The average span of a player's career in the NFL is just short of five years (4.7). For those who hit right on the average, there isn't much time to earn money. And suddenly, at the age of twenty-seven (or thirty, or thirty-five, or forty), the athlete is washed-up, over the hill, out of work.

"It was absolutely ridiculous," said Joe Morrison, who played a dozen strong seasons with the Giants, "how I went from an old veteran at thirty-three to a young head coach, one of the youngest in the country, when I retired to take the job." [Morrison had left the NFL to become coach at the University of Tennessee at Chattanooga]."

So the player must earn as much as he can as fast as he can. It makes sense. "When I went to college," said Johnson, "there were little skinny kids with glasses who were studying to be doctors and dentists and lawyers. They had to go through a long, long period of preparation, interning, clerking . . . maybe six or eight or ten years after college before they were ready to earn. But, baby, when they were ready, they were set for life. Doctors don't retire when they get to be thirty-five. Dentists don't get waived and lawyers don't get cut. Football players do.

"Suddenly, the All-America is out of work. The all-pro needs a job. He can go from earning six-figure incomes to almost nothing. There's no security and no longevity and no guarantee. It can be over tomorrow [and beginning yesterday they can limp a lot]. And doctors don't get traded, either, and have to live apart from their families [and maintain two residences] in a city they would never pick in the first place. We have to make it all in a very concentrated period of time. It's not greed, it's practicality. No one wants you to make a speech or appear in a commercial after you stop being a star."

The argument that no one twisted a football player's arm and forced him into pro football is rather weak. For some, those without the intellectual ability or desire to become doctors, lawyers, dentists, and the like, football is the only available way to earn a high income.

Most of those wise enough to recognize their position have found lifetime employment as a result of their athletic status. And that requires being out in public, meeting the wealthy fans for whom having a star on the payroll is a status symbol.

"I could try for ten years to make a sale," says a wealthy manufacturer, "but the president of that company doesn't have the time or the inclination to deal with me. But if he was a football freak, and if suddenly a guy he idolized calls for an appointment, it's like magic. So if I have a few of those stars working for me, it's good business. They'll make sales I wouldn't have a prayer of making."

Many former stars, then, find themselves in sales-related businesses when their playing careers are over. In many cases, insurance seems to be the choice field to penetrate. Al DeRogatis, a former all-pro defensive tackle with a high degree of intelligence and charm, is a vice president of the Prudential Insurance Company. He no longer sells insurance policies, but that is how he started. "I found people would buy a policy they didn't really need, or buy more insurance than they needed, because they were still impressed by my name," he said. "They were kind of stunned when I told them they didn't need something. I never liked to take advantage of my name. It just wasn't good business. But I saw it happen every day. It was easy to capitalize."

Andy Robustelli, a Hall of Fame defensive end, opened a travel agency and a sporting goods business when he retired. And he kept them when he returned to the NFL as Director of Operations for the Giants. "I never landed an appointment because of my name," he said. "When a guy would say, 'Hey, aren't you the football player?' I'd admit I was, but if I thought he didn't want to conduct business for any other reason, I turned him down. I was never a prostitute and I didn't intend to become one to earn my living. You have to have confidence in your abilities."

Recently many retired stars have found employment in other entertainment-related fields. The motion picture industry and broadcasting immediately come to mind. From sports star to movie or TV star is the story of such as Jim Brown, Tim Brown, Fred Williamson, Urban Henry, Joe Namath, O. J. Simpson, Keith-Jamaal Wilkes, Earl Monroe, Merlin Olsen, Roman Gabriel, etc., etc. On-the-job training was never so lucrative, and while the acting of most of them leaves much to be desired, the first—and most important—ingredient has already been achieved. Recognition.

"People will pay their money to see Jim Brown in a movie, just to see how he'll do," said film producer Robert Evans. "Nobody will pay to see a highly talented but unknown serious actor until he gets a 'name.' The football or sports star already has a name, and a recognizable face, too."

Others turn to television, as commentators, color analysts, or play-by-play announcers for the plethora of NFL games offered for home consumption. Frank Gifford, Alex Karras, Pat Summerall, Tom Brookshier, Don Meredith, Sonny Jurgensen, John Brodie, Paul Hornung, Emerson Boozer, Sam DeLuca, Irv Cross . . . a veritable glut on the market. Karras and Meredith, in fact, have become credible actors and are worthy of critical praise. But most are awful. It never ceases to amaze that men who played the game so well are nearly unable to explain it. And, once again, the on-the-job training program was dandy. The money never stopped flowing and qualified announcers (Keith Jackson comes to mind) were shunted off into obscurity to make room for the jocks with a name and a face.

(I once wrote a newspaper column on the shortcomings of many nationally known players-turned-broadcasters, and the mail brought volumes of insults and criticism. Chief among the fans' favorites was Gifford. Most of the knocks were from women, who demanded to know how I could criticize someone so good-looking. Clearly, it isn't what a guy says but how he looks when he's saying it. Preparation, modulation, and delivery have taken a back seat to long eyelashes and broad shoulders.)

Howard Cosell, the man people love to hate, has

spent much of his laudable professional career mocking those who have joined his field. "I never played the game," he intoned, "so how the hell could I have become so popular?" With mellifluous phraseology, he has affixed labels such as "incoherent journalism . . . mumble reporting . . . insipid favoritism . . . incompetent interviewing [and] infantile idiocy" to what many of today's most popular jocks-turned-announcers do or engage in.

Cosell also points to a player's inability to explain the game as a sure sign that the game isn't that difficult in the first place. If they all had to be brain surgeons to play football, the NFL probably would be made up of five players.

Indeed.

There was once a very effective, very large, very unintelligent defensive tackle who earned a great deal of money, popularity, and notoriety. "We don't really coach him," joked a member of his team's staff. "What we do is paint a sandwich on the opposing quarterback's helmet." Another coach, speaking about an all-pro quarterback, offered the opinion that "God must have been having a hell of a lot of fun with this one, because he gave him a million-dollar arm and a ten-cent brain."

Another defensive lineman, who came out of the Deep South with nothing but a wide streak of bigotry, was incited to riot by his coach each week. "One time I'd tell him the [opposition's] black fullback dated just white girls . . . another week I'd say the [other team's] black halfback wanted to sleep with his sister. I was always surprised when it worked."

R. C. Owens, a magnificent wide receiver and one of the first black superstars in the NFL, has told stories of attempted intimidation by the white players. "I never played a game without hearing 'nigger' a few times in pileups," he said, "and that was the most polite word I heard, too."

The general locker-room mentality is not overly elevated, which is not to say that every football player in the NFL reads only the sports statistics and comic books. But the thinkers don't last long. The intellectuals draw more than their share of suspicious glances. The questioners are quickly drummed out.

Lee Grosscup was a quarterback with long hair, and he compounded this heinous crime by enjoying the reading and writing of poetry. He was a qualified star—in college, at any rate—but his mind kept getting in the way of his teammates and his coaches. Finally, he was cut by the Giants, his first team. He was claimed by the Minnesota Vikings. Very quickly, he drew the wrath of the head coach, Norm Van Brocklin. What he did was question the game plan. "The Giants were right about you, you long-haired intellectual creep," was the Vikings' reaction. They quickly emulated the Giants and cut Grosscup again.

But the athlete as star has taken hold in the United States, and what better vehicle for such adulation than the TV commercial?

We have been witness to such perpetrations as Larry Csonka singing "It's Not Too Sweet" for a sodapop; Joe Namath discussing his personal hygiene habits with stars of other sports who are required to demonstrate impatience in order to talk about girls; Joe Namath becoming the darling of America's transvestites by modeling pantyhose; Joe Namath becoming the darling of America's gluttons by shilling popcorn machines and miniature electric hamburger and hot dog grills; O. J. Simpson running and leaping through airports to arrive, hardly out of breath, at his rent-a-car counter;

Bubba Smith ripping the tops off beer cans; Dick Butkus belittling a rugby player's "cute little shorts" for the same beer seller; Bob Griese selling men's clothing for a national department store chain; Fran Tarkenton pushing airlines; Dave Rowe proving he's human after all by extolling the virtues of stamp collecting while holding his son under his arm like a loaf of pumpernickel; Bart Starr selling a line of automobiles; and gargantuan Rosey Grier doing his needlepoint number while selling beer.

But the most objectionable of all sports stars-in-commercials-acts was left to basketball's Wilt Chamberlain, who appeared with his mother explaining how he maintained adolescent regularity.

Good Lord!

It's money, folks, not sincerity. It's a way of cashing in quickly, a way to even the score with the skinny little kid who wore glasses and is now practicing gynecology on Park Avenue. Let's bet *he* never gets an offer to sell instant iced tea on the tube. And let's bet *he* never buys it, either.

And those are merely the national commercials. You haven't begun to enjoy yourself until you've seen the local versions, with local heroes mumbling lines about local restaurants, auto dealers, banks, and men's clothing stores.

"I always buy my suits at Manny's Men's Mart, because Manny himself sews every stitch and polishes every cute little button." The star is usually seen on-screen with a buxom blond who has one arm (the one we can see) round his waist while the other arm (the one we can't see) is usually pointing at the cue cards. And Manny's Men's Mart does very nicely, thank you, even though clever Manny doesn't have a jacket in the joint that would fit the beast. If the locals think the beast shops at Manny's, that's good enough for them.

Still, there is no single area where former players are more vulnerable to embarrassment than in the broadcasting booth. And to be fair, there are minor restrictions imposed on them that do not offer much help. "We have decided," said a director for the CBS network, Sanford Grossman, "that the public doesn't want to hear too much of the technical stuff. So our analysts are told to refrain from that kind of explanation. Sometimes they slip into the language, but not often, and not nearly as much as they did, with our blessings, when this whole business first reached its peak popularity. Then, with the whole country nuts about terminology and war-words and like that, our commentators—I'm sorry, everybody's commentators, the other networks and the radio people and the newspapers, too—were heavily into the technical jargon. But the public isn't that way any more. They want descriptions in language they understand. They want to know what's going on and why it happened, and they don't want too much talking to interfere with their concentration."

Indeed, the veteran TV announcers—the play-by-play experts—have always known that there are certain requirements based on whether their medium at the moment is radio or television.

"The radio guys," Cosell said, "have to describe everything. They have to make the guy at home or in his car feel he is at the game, too, seeing the whole picture. But the TV announcers must learn not to talk to an extent . . . at least the play-by-play people. They have to remember that the fan is seeing everything they see, only better, with closeup lenses and slow motion replays. There are still basics to keep in mind like down-and-distance, the score, and how much time is left. Beyond that, the professional play-by-play man will keep it short and simple." Or, in the parlance, KISS (Keep It Simple, Stupid).

Why the heavy influx of former jocks on the air? "It's that identity factor," Grossman said. "A guy who was a great player will still attract a following, and viewers like to listen to a guy they used to follow as a player. What he says may or may not be more incisive, and he may or may not know any more than an experienced sports broadcaster, but he has a name."

There is also built-in obsolescence. For example, Kyle Rote, the all-pro player, became Kyle Rote, the national announcer and color man. He enjoyed an equal standing in the public's mind for eight years. Then, suddenly, he was gone from the picture tube. Why?

"Because as new retirements of superstars occur, the networks are anxious for this kind of fresh blood," he said. "It is probably correct that the guys who just retired know more about the game being played today and the players who are playing it. I kept up and did my homework, but there were only a handful of guys I knew personally as players. So when a guy like Jurgensen or Unitas or Meredith becomes available, the network grabs him. I knew this going in. I was never resentful. But I thought I had become a pretty fair announcer, regardless of the fact that I had been a player, too.

"I miss the work, not so much for the money but because it was a way of staying in the game, on the fringes, maybe, but still a part of football. But I understood perfectly. I knew I'd get moved out eventually. I stayed longer than most ex-athlete analysts, and I was grateful for those years. I enjoyed the hell out of it."

The television networks do, indeed, play musical

chairs with their "talent," a grossly misleading term for most announcers. The hiring of women and minority announcers has brought more confusion to the game analysis, but at least those right-place-at-the-right-time sweepstakes winners do not have to be forcibly restrained from using technical jargon.

As was the case with the scrambling quarterbacks whose peak performance years coincided with the NFL's insistence that a scrambler could never win, one wonders how many competent, erudite, and accomplished potential football announcers were sent off to disc jockey jobs in Small Town, U.S.A., in order to make room for these ex-jocks.

Again, as with the local commercials, we seldom hear local radio color commentators hired by individual teams. Generally, they are former players who earned a modicum of recognition in the cities in question, and their duties appear to be those of resident expert and head cheerleader.

A team's exhibition schedule, which is not covered by a TV network, of course, is another vehicle for local announcers, and a few weeks of exposure to such "talent" can cause even the most fervent football fan to dream of faraway beaches and lazy summer afternoons well removed from a television set or a radio.

Announcing has become too simple. When the search for the ex-athlete was set in motion at the local level, professionalism was the first quality to go. Sadly, the major networks seemed to have succumbed to the same conventional blindness. Even sadder is the fact that no one seems to care, which might prove that the game is, after all, the only important thing, and the voices can either be tolerated or blocked out.

Many fans, fed up with the chatter and one-liners ~nd parade of celebrities in evidence on the ABC

Monday night telecasts, have resorted to watching the screen with the volume off. NFL Properties, Inc., is missing a bet: Why not sell prerecorded tapes of background music to be played while watching a silent screen?

To conclude: With the advent of pro football as entertainment, we have lost a very real link between the fan and the athlete, between the fan and the team. With the added factor of unrealistic salaries, protracted court battles, and bitter labor-management disputes, we have seen a further isolation of the pro football phenomenon from the real world.

"I can't root for Larry Csonka any more," said the kid in Miami. "All he cares about is money."

When Csonka led the Dolphins Three (with Paul Warfield and Jim Kiick) from the NFL Dolphins to the rival World Football League, Miami fans were stunned. Three of their heroes had delivered a knee to the groin of an entire city's adoring populace. "I did it for security and for my family," said Csonka, who subsequently signed with the New York Giants (Warfield went to Cleveland, Kiick to Denver when the WFL drowned). "When you get an offer for that kind of money, you have no choice."

Probably. But it did point out, in bold and obvious fashion, that today's athletes have very little to do with the communities they play in. It has become a dollar chase, and the fans, most of whom harbor idealistic visions of loyalty and allegiance, are the most damaged victims of this cruel revelation.

Sports as entertainment is the current truth. No one buys a ticket to a Broadway show because the star is a hometowner. So, too, has the fan of a professional team had to adjust. He is now less concerned with the identity of a team's personnel. He has been left to root for a faceless unit, the team, because his values have been trampled upon by players such as Csonka, et al. And if those values are examined now, the cleatmarks of the 800-pound gorillas will easily be spotted.

Expansion has further diluted the credibility of athletes. There are too many teams, too many "regulars," on too many NFL rosters. "Before expansion and the AFL when there were twelve teams and only thirty-three guys on each team," remembered Gino Marchetti, a Hall of Fame defensive end from the Baltimore Colts, "everybody was a player, a legitimate player. No matter what team was on the field with you, those guys had a good chance to win the game. Today, there are guys starting who couldn't have even practiced with us. I see players who don't know how to play. Lord, would I love to be a player today. It would be so damned easy to be a superstar and get big money."

In 1959, the NFL's dozen teams contained a total of 396 players. In 1976, the NFL's twenty-eight teams contained a total of 1,204 players. Quality has suffered through diffusion and, ultimately, saturation. The least important player on a roster frequently earns more than the imposed minimum of $18,000 a year; in 1959, most of the acknowledged superstars didn't make much more than that. Clearly, the 800-pound gorilla is far from being an endangered species.

5. Is It 4-3 or 3-4 or 5-2 or Who Cares?

When John Ralston was dismissed after the 1976 season as the head coach in Denver, despite the fact that his Broncos had compiled a 9-5 record, he was asked what advice he would offer his successor, Red Miller.

"I am leaving behind two sealed envelopes in the desk of the coach's office," he said. "They are marked 'One' and 'Two.' If he loses three in a row, he is to open Envelope One, in which he will find a three-word message—'Blame Your Predecessor.'

"If he loses three more in a row, he is to open Envelope Two, in which he will find another three-word message—'Prepare Two Envelopes.' "

How to pick defensive linemen? The late Chuck Drulis, an assistant coach for many years in the NFL, offered this theory:

"I would take a group of the biggest kids I could find and lock them in a room. Then I would hit each of them a few good shots in the head. The ones who didn't mind would be offensive linemen. The ones who punched me in the mouth would be defensive linemen. If I found only three of them, I'd use a three-four defense. If I could find four linebackers. But that's another theory."

"The only thing a 'prevent' defense really prevents is winning the damned ball game," said Henry

Jordan, former all-pro defensive tackle in Green Bay. "It stinks."

Monkey-see, monkey-do was never more apparent than in the summer of 1977. Oakland was the reigning Super Bowl champion, a game it had won with a three-four defense. So during training camp, Philadelphia, Cincinnati, Miami, and Tampa Bay all went to the three-four.

The best defense is the one that stops the offense. It can have a three-man front, a four-man front, or a no-man front. On the other hand, a bad defense can have three or four or no men up front and it will still be a bad defense.

Vince Costello, an all-pro linebacker for many years and later an NFL defensive coach, was an idealist about defense. "If you do your job properly," he said, "no offensive play will gain an inch. If it does, somebody made a mistake."

On the other hand, Blanton Collier, former head coach in Cleveland (where Costello played), had another thought. "I don't care what my defense does, so long as it stops the other team from scoring. I don't care if they [the opposition's offense] can go up and down the field all day. If they start from their one-yard line and get stopped on our one-yard line, I don't mind ninety-eight-yard marches."

And so we embark upon the mysterious subject of defense in professional football. Defense is half the game, the other half being offense. Some coaches like to divide their goals into thirds by adding special team performances.

Bunk!

The special teams (kickoff and punt returns, kickoff and punt coverage) merely set things up for the offense or the defense. They are no more than adjuncts to the offense and the defense, regardless of coachly disagreement. (Aside: By placing a third of the responsibility on the special teams, or so-called suicide squads, coaches are providing themselves with another built-in copout. They can gloss over the absence of a quality offense and/or defense by fixing some of the blame to "poor coverage" or "inadequate return yardage.")

The purpose of defense is to stop the other side—the offense—from advancing the ball, extending possession by virtue of first downs and ultimately scoring. As previously stated, the best defense is the one that accomplishes this objective. Conversely, a lousy defense will be penetrated often.

How the defense is set up . . . which alignment is chosen . . . which formations are diagrammed . . . which techniques are utilized . . . all that is left to the coaching staff. Most coaches, when prodded, will acknowledge tailoring their defense (and offense) to the available personnel.

When Jack Patera was the defensive line coach of the Minnesota Vikings, his starters included Alan Page, Carl Eller, and Jim Marshall. The fourth member was either Doug Sutherland or Gary Larsen. It could almost have been Steve Cauthen.

And what pearls of wisdom did Patera have for those who wanted to investigate his success? "I make sure the guys get on the bus in time," he said.

"I also tell them . . . no, I ask them nicely . . . not to have a bad game because my family is accustomed to eating and living with a roof over their heads. I tell them which defensive maneuvers I'd like them to use, but if they wind up doing something else, that's fine.

Hey, what the hell can I teach Alan Page about playing defensive tackle? It's absurd."

And the success of the Vikings' defense—especially its front four—catapulted Patera into a position of status. He used it to become the head coach of the expansionist (1976) Seattle Seahawks. Predictably, his avowed method of building a new team began with defense. "It is at least 75 percent of the game," he said, thereby shooting all to hell the fifty-fifty party line. And he drafted for defensive personnel. And the 1976 Seahawks, while generally atrocious, had a reasonably effective defense. After all, it was a team designed around the available personnel . . . which happened to be mostly defensive.

Patera, who also leaned heavily on defense when he conducted the Seahawks' stocking draft from available NFL veterans, was light years ahead of the other expansion team in 1976, Tampa Bay. Seattle had a 2-12 record while Tampa Bay established a league mark for incompetence by losing all fourteen games, and Seattle outscored the Buccaneers by more than one hundred points.

Seattle came within six points of beating St. Louis (30-24) in the opening game, which ended with the Seahawks on the Cardinals' one-yard line as the clock ran out. Seattle also fell six points short of an upset of Minnesota (27-21) and that, according to Patera, was "the worst I felt all season." He had wanted to beat his former team badly, and surprised the nation by coming as close to that goal as he did. Which led to a question.

"Jack, did your team have that kind of success against the Vikings because you knew the Minnesota defense?"

The answer was delightfully direct and brief: "You bet your ass," he said with a smile.

All right, you are about to build a defense. Which route will you take? Do you go for size? Quickness? Emphasis on stopping the pass? The run? Do you like a three-man front? Four? Are you into zone coverage in the secondary? Man-to-man? A combination thereof? Do you want swift, agile linebackers? Big, bulky ones? Three of them? Four?

As you can see, there are a lot of questions to be asked, and an equal number of answers to be given before this task can be accomplished. But do not fall into the trap of predetermination. It is far better to do the designing after you have seen the athletes—far smarter to tailor the defense to the bodies.

Hank Stram, who built a machine in Kansas City and began the same type of construction work in New Orleans in 1976, has a view of defense worth repeating. "It is best to put a defense into military terms," he said, "since this is, after all, war simulation. The front line is the infantry. They are to let nothing get past them . . . at least, not without slowing down the attackers.

"The linebackers are the tank corps. They must be able to move quickly to the area of attack . . . they must be strong enough to drive over obstacles . . . and they must be clever enough not to get bogged down in unnecessary traffic.

"Finally, the secondary is like the anti-aircraft units. When the offense throws the ball, after the infantry has been stopped and the tanks neutralized, the deep backs are the final line of defense. Those backs must be rangy and quick, smart and fearless. They must intimidate the receivers. Every receiver is taught that the most important part of his job is total concentration on his pattern and the ball. But a man has to lose a little of that concentration if he's concerned about his health.

Sometimes the deep backs get their job done even if the receiver catches the ball. If they punish him enough, he'll remember it the next time."

For the sake of expedience, let our first defense be built with four front linemen, three linebackers, and four deep backs (two cornerbacks, two safeties). This is what is known in the trade as a four-three. You will need two defensive ends and two defensive tackles, and it will be suggested that your quicker men be placed at the end positions. Generally, the ends have no one to their outside, which allows them the freedom to go wide and swoop back in to find the quarterback. But caution: If your end isn't quick enough, he won't get back inside fast enough and as a result he won't be able to do the job.

(Many NFL ends weigh no more than linebackers. Fred Dryer of the Los Angeles Rams, for instance, plays down to 220 during a season, yet he has been an all-pro several times.)

The heavier, slower linemen are the tackles. They should have more straight-ahead strength than the ends, for they have to work their way through the guards, the center, and, often at least one blocking back before they can inflict harm to the quarterback. Putting a natural tackle at end is just as ill-advised as putting a natural end at tackle. The positions are not the same, although there are those who can play either one—athletes gifted not only with size and strength, but speed and quickness.

The basic advantage of a four-man line is that it provides another pass rusher and another potential tackler at the line of scrimmage. The great defenses of the past twenty years have all been four-three alignments—Baltimore and the New York Giants of the 1950s . . . Green Bay, the Giants, Los Angeles, and

Chicago of the 1960s . . . Dallas, Pittsburgh, and Minnesota of the 1970s.

There were, however, two small changes in the early seventies. They occurred in Miami and in Washington, and each provided a base for the others to build on. Miami, under the direction of defensive coach Bill Arnsparger, took to removing a down lineman and inserting a fourth linebacker, Bob Matheson. The formation was called a fifty-three, for no other reason than Matheson's jersey number was 53. Matheson had the strength to act as a down lineman if the play developed into a run, and the quickness of a linebacker to cover downfield against a pass attempt. It worked wondrously well, and provided the final impetus that turned the Miami defense into a championship unit, which reached its zenith with a perfect 17-0 season in 1972.

In Washington, clever George Allen, the head coach who built the 1960s defensive monsters in Chicago, came up with a fifth defensive back, who was inserted to replace either a linebacker or a down lineman. This was called the Nickel Defense, and it, too, resulted in a plethora of big plays that took the Redskins to several championship games and one Super Bowl—against Miami.

Then along came teams such as Houston and New England, whose coaches reacted to the fact that they didn't have four decent down linemen. What they did was play only three of them along with an extra linebacker. That, fans, is the three-four. Terminology allows for the down linemen to be called ends (there are two of those) and middle guard or nose tackle (a relative of the "nose guard" used by many college defenses). Accordingly, there are two outside linebackers and two inside linebackers. Most frequently the quicker athletes are the outside linebackers, and their job is to assist on pass coverage and to help "string out" sweeps. Bulkier, stronger, and no doubt slower linebackers become the inside men, whose primary duties involve assisting the front linemen against the run and knocking down any receiver who dares threaten to catch a ball in the middle of the field.

Some coaches believe that the three-four shores up pass defense, while being somewhat weak against the run, but by 1977 most teams used occasional formations designed exactly that way. In that year, several coaches also turned to an interesting off-shoot of this philosophy—they brought in a fourth down lineman in pass situations, taking out one of the linebackers to create a spot for the fifth defensive back.

One of these days, if they aren't careful, they'll find themselves with the old four-three alignment in a certain passing situation, and they might even discover it works.

But in January of 1977 the Oakland Raiders won the Super Bowl with a three-four defense and did not allow the Minnesota Vikings to do much either on the ground or in the air.

How come?

The personnel.

The Vikings had decided to run against the three-four. They also decided that a sufficient number of play-fake passes, in which the quarterback pretends to hand the ball off to a running back but then pulls it away and passes downfield, would work because the four linebackers would be frozen for an all-important split second. So they entered the game with many running plays and many play-fake passes (also called play-action passes) and were saddened to discover that Oakland's personnel was good enough to play a three-four defense and not get burned by either runs or passes.

Most of the credit lies with the four linebackers: Phil Villapiano and Ted Hendricks on the outside, Monte Johnson and Willie Hall on the inside. Villapiano and Hendricks took care of the sweeps. Johnson and Hall plugged the holes and filled the gaps, to stop inside runs, as well as adding to the pass rush against the Minnesota's quarterback, Fran Tarkenton. In addition, all four linebackers were adept at dropping back to assume short pass-coverage roles. The Vikings were strapped. They were without alternatives.

It was suggested later that a simple change in the offensive blocking technique might have defeated the three-four. If the interior line had been more concerned with "slip blocking" rather than the more primary hit-and-hold blocks, the center or a lead back could have gone out to seal off one of the inside linebackers. Or one of the tackles might have been freed (by a guard-center or guard-back double-team) to fire out and neutralize one of the outside linebackers.

There is, after all, an apparent advantage to the offense that is faced with a three-four defense. At the snap of the ball, there is one less man to block on the line of scrimmage. As a result, there has to be an offensive lineman not burdened with his usual assignment. But the Vikings chose to follow the inaccurate theory of running away from the three-man front and utilizing many play-fake passes. Oakland had seen that theory utilized all season. Oakland had also lost only one game all season.

"When they allow you to overload your offensive line," offered Allie Sherman, "by giving you an extra lineman, you should be able to capitalize on that and force them out of the defense they want to play." That, truly, is the basic theory of football. If the defense can force the offense into changing its plans, it will win. And if the offense can force the defense into compensatory action, it will win.

In Super Bowl XI, Minnesota allowed Oakland to stay in its three-four. Moreover, it allowed the Raiders to do what they did best by putting no particular pressure on them to change. What the Vikings did was play directly into the Raiders' hands. Even the Raiders were somewhat surprised.

And the coaches have a cliché for this failing, too. "You dance with who brung you," it goes. And it means you do exactly the same things you have done all season, since they worked best and got you to a championship game in the first place. This disinclination, or inability, to change can always be exploited by the most astute coaching staffs. And it always is.

Whether it is easier to run against a three-four or pass against a four-three is problematical, at best. Most students of professional football continue to insist that personnel and the proper execution of assignments will always be a key factor. A quarterback will find it difficult to pass if he is wearing a defensive tackle in his navel, and whether that tackle emerged from a three- or four-man line is immaterial to the quarterback. It still hurts. And the pass will still be aborted.

In pro football's early days—and, indeed, as late as the early 1950s—the teams usually employed five-man defensive lines. This put great pressure on the offensive lineman and the quarterback, but left the middle area of the field far more vulnerable. And as offenses began to place more and more emphasis on the passing aspect of the game, defensive coaches realized there was a need for a new deployment of their eleven men.

Hence, one of the five front linemen dropped back

to join the two linebackers. So was born the four-three. It was as simple as that. When the five-man line was used, the guy in the middle was called, creatively, the middle guard, just as the man in the middle on today's three-man line is called the nose tackle. It's just that instead of two mates on either side he has only one to his left and one to his right.

This, too, must be noted: It is usually difficult to definitely identify a three-four or a four-three because nothing in pro football is that black and white. The only way to know what formation is being used is to watch the players, because often the fourth linebacker will actually play up on the line and act like a down lineman. More frequently used is the specialized defense when a formation is ordered for a particular situation. "We'll use a fifth back on sure pass," said Allen. "We'll also use a fifth back if we want them to run."

There are, however, some innovators. Dallas' coach Tom Landry is one of them. He is also one of the few head coaches in the game who is equally adept at theorizing on offense or defense. His record with Dallas proves his expertise.

Landry uses a defensive formation he calls "the Flex." In the Flex, designed with the basic four-three as its root formation, one end or tackle is positioned a yard or two off the line of scrimmage. The basic theory behind this is that blocking assignments will be made more difficult because at least one offensive lineman will have to "go get" the targeted defender; and once that happens, gaps will open through which the linebackers can shoot.

It might be added, however, that with such linemen as Randy White (and Bob Lilly before that), Jethro Pugh, Harvey Martin, and Ed "Too Tall" Jones, Landry's Flex had a far better chance of working than if he had three turkeys and a stiff to deal with.

When the linebackers shoot the gaps, that is known as blitzing or red-dogging. In its simplistic terms, it offers another challenge to the offensive line, since an agile man who weighs, say, 230 and has a five- to ten-yard head start, can suddenly hurtle through a hole and can zoom in on the quarterback.

Shooting or blitzing or red-dogging became popular as offenses began to rely more and more on the pass. There are probably more variations of the blitz than there are kinds of defenses. Any blitz puts additional pressure on the center, who otherwise could be of help to either guard on a two-man block, and/or on the backs, one or both of whom now must be able and successful blockers. It is the center or a blocking back who must "pick up" the blitz.

Such antics also resulted in a colorful term for an offensive block. It was named by Green Bay offensive linemen after a particularly hellish Thanksgiving Day game against Detroit in 1962 in which the Lions sacked quarterback Bart Starr eleven times.

"It was our 'Lookout' block," recalled all-pro guard Jerry Kramer. "How it worked was this way: Detroit would send a couple of linebackers through and we'd get all worked up about them and forget the front four and somehow somebody was always penetrating and sitting on Bart's chest. Being aware of the public's love affair with terminology, we called it our Lookout block. As the guy got past us, we'd turn to Starr and yell: 'Look out, Bart, I missed him.' But old Bart was usually too preoccupied to answer us at the time. We heard from him after the game, though. I never knew he used language like that."

The "Lookout," by the way, is cousin to a block

that came to be known as the "Fuckit" in Miami. It involved the Dolphins' all-pro heart of the line—center Jim Langer and guards Larry Little and Bob Kuechenberg—and all-pro fullback Larry Csonka. It was born on a Monday night in 1974, against the Cincinnati Bengals, in a game won by Miami, 24-3. Late in the fourth quarter, with the outcome long since decided, Csonka took a handoff and shot through the middle for twenty-four yards. An enterprising newspaperman approached Langer after the game, twitted on about how impressed he was with that play, and asked Langer to explain it to him. Langer smiled.

"What happened was I missed my block, Little missed his block, and Kuechenberg missed his, and when Zonk got to the line of scrimmage I yelled: 'Zonk, we missed 'em all.' Zonk had a full head of steam going, and I swear I hear him scream: 'Fuckit.' Then he made twenty-four. That's how the play worked. Got it?"

Got it.

The coaches don't talk about Lookout or Fuckit blocks, but there is a suspicion they happen at least as often as the ones that are supposed to happen. Defense is meant to intimidate. If it does, half the battle is won. And few defenses were ever as intimidating as the New York Giant units of the 1950s and early 1960s . . . especially to a rookie quarterback.

In 1961, Norm Snead was a rookie quarterback with the hopelessly incompetent Washington Redskins, and he remembered a game that season in Yankee Stadium. The Giants won it, 53-0. Snead was tackled twice for safeties and was sacked ten times in all.

"I will never forget it," he said years later. "I remember getting down behind the center and starting to call the signals. I looked over the middle and there was Sam Huff . . . just grinning at me. I looked away, and there was [end] Jim Katcavage, with a kind of eerie, glassy look in his eyes. I turned to look in the other direction, and there was Andy Robustelli [the other end] and I swear he was drooling. And then I knew . . . I just knew . . . that my line wasn't about to block out all those killers. I got a funny feeling in the pit of my stomach that I'll never forget, either."

Intimidation . . .

Al DeRogatis was an all-pro defensive tackle for New York in the early 1950s, and would have played many more than four seasons if a serious knee injury had been properly treated. The Giants were playing the Philadelphia Eagles in a game that really didn't matter. Both teams were out of the running, it was late in the season, and even the game had been decided, with the Giants well ahead in the fourth quarter.

The Giants had the ball. The handoff went to a rookie running back. When the play was stopped, Eagle tackle Bucko Kilroy, one of the "overly aggressive" players of his day, cracked the unsuspecting rookie across the side of the face with a gigantic forearm. The kid went down as if shot, and suffered a multiple fracture of the jaw. "I asked Bucko what the hell he did that for," DeRogatis remembered. "I said the game didn't matter and the season was over and what was the sense of it all?

"He looked at me and seemed hurt. 'The kid will be back next season,' he said, 'and now I know he'll remember me.' "

Intimidation . . .

David "Deacon" Jones was one of the finest defensive ends in the history of the game. He stood six six and he weighed 250 or so, and he had the uncanny quickness of a panther. Pete Gent, a 200-pound wide receiver for the Dallas Cowboys, remembered a day when he found himself at tight end in "one of Landry's whacko offenses." And he found himself opposite Deacon Jones in a play that called for the tight end to block out the defensive end.

"Ol' Deac just kinda looked at me real surprised, you know? Then he started grinnin' and laughin' and finally he said: 'Hey, junior, you gonna block me?' Shit, I knew I wasn't gonna block him and he knew I wasn't gonna block him, and I just wish somebody had told Landry there was no way I coulda blocked him. He blew past me so fast I only saw the back of his jersey. I damn near got the quarterback killed."

Intimidation . . .

It was January 12, 1969, and the belittled New York Jets were going to play the awesome Baltimore Colts in Super Bowl III. The Colts, then part of the NFL (before the agreed-upon NFL-AFL merger was put into effect) were prohibitive favorites. A Jet fan could have gotten an eighteen-point handicap. But were the Jets awed by it all?

On the first play of the game, Baltimore running back Tom Matte gained a few yards and was tackled by Jet linebacker Larry Grantham. "Nice tackle," said Matte, arising.

"Up yours," said Grantham, grinning. The Jets won the game, in what must still be considered the most dramatic upset of all time.

Intimidation . . .

Baltimore had a defensive lineman named Eugene Lipscomb, better known as Big Daddy. The late Lipscomb was six seven and weighed 310. Nobody was ever meaner.

In a game against Detroit in 1959, Big Daddy realized he was matched against a rookie offensive lineman. Before the first play, he stared across the line into the rookie's eyes. "Hey, boy," he said, "which leg you want me to snap?" Lipscomb had three sacks in the first quarter, after which the rookie lineman was replaced.

Intimidation (with humor) . . .

Joe Perry was one of the greatest fullbacks ever. He played for San Francisco, and in one game against the Giants he was merciless in breaking tackles and ribs. Finally, the 49ers neared the goal line and Perry got the ball. He charged through the line—head-first into the goal post, which in those days was on the goal line, not on the back line of the end zone. He immediately knocked himself unconscious.

A few moments later, when he awoke, the first face he saw belonged to Jimmy Patton, the Giants' gutsy little safety. "You run past me again," Patton snarled, "and I'll cold-cock you again."

Visibly shaken, Perry staggered off the field and over to coach Red Strader. "Did you see that little sumbitch hit me?" he asked. "That guy's murder." Strader laughed. "It was the goal post, you dummy," he said. "It's a good thing you hit it with your head."

Intimidation can take on uglier aspects, too. R. C. Owens, one of the finest wide receivers, recalled his first season in the NFL in the 1950s when he was one of the league's first blacks. " I must have heard the word 'nigger' a hundred times," said this marvelously gifted athlete. "It was always used to try to upset me. It never did. Finally, some of the defensive backs got around to apologizing, saying, 'Hell, R. C., we had to see if we could scare you outta this league.' "

The bottom line is simply this: Intimidation usually works best when accompanied by a shattering blow to the opponent's body or a threat of such an act. You

tional college power. And because Oklahoma was virtually unbeatable, Bud's five-two was quickly copied by most of the other defensive-minded coaches in the country. Hence, it became known as the Oklahoma defense. The pro folks sneered. "It's weak against the run," said some of them. "It's weak against the pass," mumbled others.

Then Greasy Neale, the head coach of the Eagles, tried it. For the first time, an NFL defense showed four deep backs. It worked. It was neither weak against the run nor against the pass. So everybody else used it and it became known as the Eagle defense.

It was the same thing as the Oklahoma defense.

Before the Eagle, the NFL teams had fooled with a five-three, utilizing a middle linebacker three decades before Sam Huff, Joe Schmidt, Bill George, and Ray Nitschke became famous. That was called the Giant Defense (right, because the Giants had tried it first under Steve Owen, who had copied it from a Temple coach named John DaGrosa). Soon it became the only defense used in the NFL, and it remained entrenched for a decade, until the mid-1940s.

It began to fade when offensive coaches started to send the running backs out on pass patterns, for a tightly bunched five-three wasn't capable of covering diverse pass routes. So much for the five-three.

This leads to discussion of pro football's version of the age-old question, "Which came first, the chicken or the egg?" In football, it goes like this: "Does the offense dictate to the defense or does the defense dictate to the offense?" The answers one receives depends on whether one is talking to a man with offensive or defensive inclinations.

"The offensive team has an obligation to take whatever the defense is giving away that day," said Fran

Tarkenton. "No defense is perfect. There is always a flaw, a crack, a seam. You have to find it. Then you can force the defense into making adjustments. And then you have them coming and going."

Tarkenton always enjoyed keying his passing game around the movements of the free safety. "If he came up, the receiver kept going behind him, and if he dropped back, the receiver pulled up short and caught the ball in front of him. It always works." Sounds easy, doesn't it? It is.

But Y. A. Tittle was a master of that when Tarkenton was still a schoolboy in Georgia. In 1962, the Giants were playing the Eagles. Tittle was the New York quarterback. An unfortunate soul named Claude Crabbe was the Philadelphia safety. and Y. A. did a cruel thing. He sent split end (the term wide receiver had not yet become fashionable) Del Shofner on a deep left-to-right crossing pattern. He sent flanker Frank Gifford on a deep right-to-left crossing pattern. The point on the field where the two receivers crossed was directly in front of poor Claude Crabbe. He was damned if he did and damned if he didn't. If he went for Gifford, Shofner was clear. If he went for Shofner, Gifford was the hero.

It worked and it worked and it worked, and finally Gifford, a man of profound compassion, felt moved to help Claude Crabbe. "As we crossed, I yelled at him, 'It's Shofner, it's Shofner.' And it was. But he was so paranoid by then he thought I was lying, so he went to cover me. And Shofner got another touchdown pass."

The point is this: What if some knuckle-dragging behemoth of a defensive lineman had played José Greco on one of the Giant linemen's chests and deposited Tittle on his ass? Gifford and Shofner could have crossed deep patterns all day and achieved nothing more than strong leg muscles. And when the game was over, Claude Crabbe could have smiled and said: "Those two turkeys didn't catch a ball against me all afternoon. Gifford and Shofner, my ass."

Tittle was able to take what the Eagle defense gave him because he recognized what it could not do. It wasn't Crabbe's fault. Tittle had too much time to throw. The Eagles gave the Giants everything. The Giants' offensive linemen took it all by blocking out the defensive chargers.

The other side of the coin: "There are certain quarterbacks in this league who can be beaten by letting them throw," said Vince Costello, a linebacker of several Pro Bowl years with Cleveland. "We defend hard against the run and make them pass."

What Vince was too polite to say is that he considered certain NFL quarterbacks horseshit passers.

Horseshit.

Any quarterback who has earned a spot on an NFL team is capable of completing a pass. That is a purely mechanical activity. It requires no thinking . . . no brilliant strategical chess moves . . . no dabbling in the occult. Man is open, throw the damned ball to him, man will catch it. What Costello really meant is that by stopping the run, he was forcing the quarterback to pass. And when a defense knows the offense has to pass, it will become increasingly more difficult to do that.

"I remember the 1961 championship game," said Greg Larson, who was a rookie offensive tackle that year with New York before embarking on a long and glorious career as an all-pro center. "We fell behind early to the Packers [indeed, the final score was 37-0], and after a while they knew we had to pass and then they simply ignored our running game and came in swinging fists and elbows and yelling and looking crazy in the eyes. It was the most frightening thing I ever saw in a football game. Play after play, pounding and slapping and punching. It was enough to make a man cry from the physical brutality of it all."

It might be said that the Packers chose to make the Giants pass. Nonsense. The Green Bay offense put the Giants in a hole, and then the Giants had to pass in order to catch up. Y. A. Tittle was the Giants' quarterback that day, and a secondary composed of four Claude Crabbes wouldn't have helped him at all. This, then, is what truly dictates in football: the score.

If one team is far ahead, the other team's offense must take extraordinary steps to catch up. When that happens, the defense can react to the sudden-strike emphasis and defeat it. Conversely, when a team is ahead, its offense does not have to pass. So it can lull the defense to sleep by running the ball. That will draw the defenders closer, for they must force a punt in order to get their offense back on the field again.

And when a defense is drawn up close, nothing in the world will work as well as a play-action, play-fake pass. Like on third-and-inches. But few offenses have the imagination to call such plays.

Bart Starr did. He became famous as the shiftiest sumbitch ever to play quarterback in the NFL. Vince Lombardi was his coach, and Vince Lombardi was not ultra-conservative, you see. Old Vince liked his surprises as well as the next coach. He just didn't believe in taking unnecessary chances.

And so when the Packers held a lead, or even trailed, and when they were around the middle of the field, and when it came up to third-and-one, a sneaky little smile would impose itself on Vince Lombardi's jowls. And that same sneaky little smile would next be seen on the faces of the ten offensive players waiting for Starr's call in the huddle. And Starr would be absolutely immersed in mirth.

And very briskly they'd clap their hands and break the huddle and get into position and Starr would put the ball into Jim Taylor's rock-hard belly and then he'd take it back while a crazed defense tore the big fullback to shreds. And in sudden alarm they'd realize Taylor didn't have the ball. And too late they'd see Starr fading back and looking downfield, and there would be Max McGee or Boyd Dowler or Carroll Dale drifting way out there, all alone, and powerless they'd watch the ball spiral out of Bart's hand and fly with relentless accuracy into the hands of the uncovered receiver. And instead of a one-touchdown lead it was a two-touchdown lead, and the game, as they say, was in the fridge.

The offense dictates to the other offense. And the defenses do what they have to do. That is too simple. The coaches will never buy it.

6. Don't Lose Your Playbook

Most teams have a $500 fine ready for those players who lose or misplace their playbooks. This indicates the dramatic increase in the cost of notebook paper. A more realistic fine would be $2.98. That's just about the value of the binder. The rest is worthless.

When Ray Nitschke did his middle linebacker's act for the Green Bay Packers—and there have seldom been more violent or successful middle linebackers— the thing he dreaded most was the weekly written test administered by head coach Vince Lombardi. Each player had to submit to a test on the plays in the book and the plays involved in the coming Sunday's game plan. Lombardi always returned Nitschke's efforts covered with red ink. The only answers he had right were those he guessed. But every Sunday Nitschke would play an all-pro game.

Then Nitschke, a notoriously free-thinking bachelor, got married. Suddenly his test papers were perfect, but his play suffered badly.

"Nitschke," boomed Lombardi, "I wish you'd break up this marriage of yours."

"Why, coach?" asked the incredulous Nitschke.

"Because when you were single and sleeping on park benches and getting drunk, you never had the answers right but you played like hell. Now that wife of yours is making you study. So you get the answers right, and you're playing like an old woman." So much for playbooks.

"I never looked much at the playbook, and I never did pay much attention to the game plans," Nitschke said after embarking on retirement. "What the hell, football is instinctive. Especially defensive football. You don't have time to stop and think about where you should be or what your responsibilities are or where the other guys are going. Bullshit. You follow the ball and you find which of those motherfuckers has it, and then you make them sorry they took the damned thing from the quarterback.

"And receivers? Oh, Lord, did I love receivers. Especially the brave morons who came across the middle into my territory. A receiver is kind of vulnerable, you know. He's watching the quarterback or he's looking for the ball and that means he has to pay no attention to me. And that's a fatal mistake, because I'm going to hit him as hard as I can and if he can still hold the ball, I'll hit him harder next time. Now how the hell can anybody put that in a playbook."

Bill Arnsparger, who spent two full seasons and half of a third as the head coach of the New York Giants, was a taciturn, almost reluctant speaker. But there were times when he slipped and inadvertently gave away too many trade secrets. During his half-season in 1976, while studying film in preparation for a game against Los Angeles, he had the chance to break down the Rams' previous game, a 10-10 stalemate with the Minnesota Vikings. The game had been a study in defensive fury. Over the span of five full quarters—the only way an NFL game can result in a tie—each team was able to manage just one touchdown.

The big plays were defensive plays, and since Arnsparger's one, and only, real skill was as a defensive as-

sistant and tactician, he was understandably enthusi-
astic at these beautifuly executed maneuvers. In the
overtime quarter, the Vikings were moving toward
what appeared to be a game-ending touchdown. They
were at the Rams' ten-yard line when quarterback
Fran Tarkenton faded back to pass. It was a pass intercepted by a Los Angeles linebacker, Rick Kay. Arnsparger beamed. "Los Angeles concentrates on its
defense," he said, "and Kay played it perfectly. He was
in what we call I-coverage. He made a perfect drop
and got into a perfect position and just waited. Tarkenton had to arc the ball over his head. He didn't. Kay
intercepted the ball. But Francis had called a nice play,
too. It was what we call a Q-pattern, a kind of curl to
the outside in the end zone."

In one statement, Arnsparger had underlined the
fact and fabric of coaching. The Rams' defense was in
"what we call I-coverage" and the Vikings' pass receiver, rookie Sammy White, had run "what we call a
Q-pattern."

Arnsparger smiled (well, almost smiled). "Basically," he admitted, "the offenses and defenses in the
league are the same. The differences are in the various
techniques used within the offensive play or the defensive strategy. How you play it is one obvious difference. It could be the same defensive set, for instance,
but are you playing it to the inside, outside, or head-
up? That's important.

"Say you're calling a running play. It might be iden-
tical," he continued, "to a running play the Rams use,
or the Vikings. Or any other team. But how do you
block it out? The runner is going to take the same
angle to hit the same hole, but that's just one part of it.
Do you cross-block or pull-block or zone-block? There
will always be differences, because you must tailor your

offense and defense to the type of personnel you have. If you have big, quick linebackers, you do certain things and hope they're done well. If you have smaller or slower linebackers, you try to do other things."

Arnsparger even admitted that Tom Landry, the head coach of the Dallas Cowboys and the one man rumored to be the most innovative, doesn't really do anything new.

"The things the Cowboys use just aren't used by most other clubs," Arnsparger said. "That doesn't mean the others couldn't do what the Cowboys do. It's a matter of needing the right personnel . . . or even trying to cover up for certain weaknesses. Why do some teams blitz so frequently on defense? Because they either don't have a very good rush line or their deep backs can't cover very well. You're always trying to compensate for a weakness.

"Dallas is the only team to play the Flex defense at the moment," Arnsparger continued. "But it's not a new thing, and it's not difficult to put in or coach. It's just a matter of choice. You have to spend a lot of time with it when you put it in . . . like with anything different . . . and it has to be a real commitment. You have to start it from day one of summer camp, and you can't suddenly scrap it if it's not working well early in the season. But hell, Tom was using that Flex when he was an assistant coach with the Giants in the fifties. He's just put some different wrinkles in it now, staggered the front guys more.

"His offense, too, isn't new or anything like that. It's a short punt formation, or a shotgun formation, or even a single-wing set with one less back than they used with the single-wing forty years ago. We could go into it with a simple call in the huddle. Then we could run a play off it by simply calling one of our regular plays. It doesn't take much to line up in a different way. It's what you, as the coach, feel is best for the team and the personnel.

"You don't want to clutter up the playbook," he added, "with stuff you don't expect to use much. So we don't have a shotgun play drawn up, but we do have the terminology. It's all what you want to do, and any coach can teach any kind of formation."

Indeed.

Given a blackboard and a stick of chalk, any of the head coaches or assistant coaches in the National Football League can diagram and fully explain any other team's offense or defense; moreover, they can then go right into a tangential explanation of how to best defense that offense, or attack that defense.

"When Landry and I were both assistants with the Giants," Allie Sherman recalled, "we'd work as a team. I was the offensive coordinator and he was the defensive coordinator. He'd come up with an idea for a particular defensive alignment. He'd draw it on the blackboard. Then I'd attack it, point out all its strong points and weak points. If I found too many ways to hurt it, he wouldn't use it.

"I had the same respect for his defensive knowledge. If I put an offense on the board and told him how the play was designed to work, he'd start to build a defense against it. If he thought it would be too easy to stop, I'd forget about it. But Tom was an outstanding defensive coach.

"He'd know how to stop an offensive formation I used and nobody else was able to think of the solution. But it was there for anyone to see. All they had to do was know enough about defense . . . or offense. I mean, when there are only eleven men and only one football, how the hell can anything be new after all this time? Nothing is new. Surprise and execution are the only two factors that count any more."

Surprise and execution. "Just execution," said Vince Lombardi. "Surprises are for losers."

During Lombardi's glory years with the Packers, the most glorious and famous of all the Green Bay offensive plays was a sweep. It has been remembered, variously, as the Green Bay Sweep or the Packer Sweep or the Lombardi Sweep. It was a study in simplicity. Contrary to the NFL's propaganda department, you see, there just might be a few players around who don't understand quantuum theory or who may not be conversant with Kant and Einstein.

"Our sweep was so simple I could teach it to a sportswriter," kindly old Vince once said. "But what the hell, sportswriters might be the only ones not to grasp it." With such a heavy load of guilt, we will nevertheless attempt to describe the Lombardi Sweep.

First of all, there was absolutely nothing spectacular about Lombardi's sweep. It was usually run to the right side—because most pro football teams are "right-handed," which means a high percentage of all running plays will go to the right. Why? Because either the fullback or the halfback was eligible to carry the ball. Lombardi's two backs were Jim Taylor, the fullback, and Paul Hornung, the halfback. Both worked it with uncommon success.

The blocking was drawn up to utilize both guards, the tight end, and the non-carrying running back at the point of attack. The guards pulled to their right, which required a rather strenuous run by the left guard in order to get there in time. "I know it's a difficult maneuver," Lombardi said. "But he has to get there. I don't give a damn whether he enjoys getting there or not." Once there, the left guard and the right guard form the primary blocking wall. The non-carrying back is responsible for driving up off right tackle, going through the line of scrimmage, and blocking on the defensive tackle. The near-guard (right guard) must block on the cornerback. The far-guard has to choose between the middle linebacker or the outside linebacker. The tackles block straight ahead and seal their victims, shielding them from the ball with their bodies. All other members of the offense have specific duties as well, although the quarterback's job is done when he makes the handoff.

"You think there's anything special about this sweep?" Lombardi said. "Well, there isn't. It's as basic a play as there can be in football. We simply do it over and over and over.

"Football players are no different from real people. They learn better through repetition, constant repetition. There can never be enough emphasis on repetition. I want my players to be able to run this sweep in their sleep. Over and over and over. If we call the sweep twenty times, I'll expect it to work twenty times . . . not eighteen, not nineteen. We do it often enough in practice so that no excuse can exist for screwing it up."

As simple as this play was in concept, that simple was it to defense. But knowing that it was coming and then being able to stop it were seldom tied together by logic.

"That fucking sweep worked because everybody on the team did his job," said the late Don McCafferty, an assistant and later head coach with the Baltimore Colts and Detroit Lions. "The Packers had great players. The guards were superb, the running backs, the quarterback. It was merely execution, and the defenses were the ones to get executed. Mysterious? Not a chance. Just too damned good."

When the Packers needed an advance, they went to the Lombardi Sweep. "It was our bread and butter play, our lead item," Lombardi recalled. "Every team in the league had a sweep like that. It was a relic from single-wing football. We just used it more efficiently."

But if the Green Bay players played for another team, and were as well-coached, the Lombardi Sweep would have worked just as well. But it wouldn't have been called the Lombardi Sweep, of course.

"Coaching is kind of an overrated business," said former American Football League player Tom Beer. "There are only so many things you can do with a football. All the coaches know those things. It's their players and their luck that makes some of them winners and some losers. But no coach stays lucky forever, or has good players all the time. The day a coach signs a contract, he has set in motion his firing. All that's left to do is figure out when the next press conference should be called."

The first thing a new head coach does is assemble his playbook. "When I was coaching," boasted George Halas, "my athletes had to learn five hundred plays."

"Bullshit," said Dick Butkus, who played for Papa Bear, "there just aren't that many plays in the world. What old George did was count every variation of a play as a new one. I'd guess the offense had about twenty plays, and the defense had about ten formations. Period."

Once upon a time, a quarterback of little ability decided to get even when cut by his umpteenth team. He offered the playbook around the league. There were no takers.

"What would we do with the Saints' playbook, even

assuming we were interested in that kind of thing?" asked Oakland's Managing General Partner, Al Davis. "Once I figured out the numbering system, which would take about ten minutes, I'd find all our plays or ones we decided not to use."

What will be found in a pro playbook, then, is an outline, a description of the basic plays the coaching staff has settled on to make the most of the unique qualities of the players.

"You may see plays in the book and never use them once all season," said Beer. "There may be plays, on the other hand, that are used every game . . . many, many times in every game. Sometimes, when you see another team use a play that works, you say to yourself, 'Hey, we have that sucker, why don't we use it?' That's called questioning your coach. That's not a nice thing to do, especially if you say it out loud and the coach hears you.

"You see, he's very concerned with calling the right plays, if he actually calls them for the quarterback, or for giving the quarterback the right combinations of plays. This is the easier way, because if the team gets squashed, the coach can tell the quarterback he called the wrong plays. If the coach does it himself, who is there for him to blame?"

A momentary aside: When a quarterback named Lee Grosscup was released by the Giants in 1962, he went to the Vikings. When Norm Van Brocklin, then the Vikings' head coach, saw Grosscup's long hair, he was released by the Vikings, too. Van Brocklin didn't like longhairs or poets or other quarterbacks, the reason being that he was once a great quarterback and couldn't tolerate either inferiority or mimicry.

So Grosscup, at loose ends, accepted a telephone call from a man named Bulldog Turner. Bulldog's job then was to act as head coach of the old New York Titans of the American League until the team could find a real one.

"Lee, we are out here in Oakland and I'd like you to consider playing for us," said Turner.

"I considered it. I will," said Grosscup, clearly a man able to make snap decisions.

"That's great, Lee. Thanks. Take a plane out here as soon as you can, and I'll pick you up at the airport."

Which Grosscup did. Which Bulldog did.

And now we pick up the story in a taxicab.

"Lee," Bulldog is saying, "I'd like you to play for us. Tonight."

"Tonight?" mumbled the suddenly subdued Grosscup.

"Tonight," repeated Bulldog. "What do you need to know?"

Grosscup scrambled. "Well, some of the running plays would be nice. And a few of the pass patterns. And the names of some of the guys I'm going to be playing with, I suppose."

Bulldog outlined a sketchy sequence of running and passing plays. He also said things like Bill and Pat and Dan and Art and Norm and Dick. Then Grosscup asked about audibles.

"Audibles?" said Bulldog, obviously stumped.

"Yeah, audibles . . . automatics . . . like when I want to change a play at the line of scrimmage," Grosscup explained, while wondering just what sort of a league this AFL really was.

Bulldog blanched. "Goddammit, Grosscup, Van Brocklin was right about you. Don't you ever change a play at the line of scrimmage. Never."

Let us now examine playbooks. "They are a working tool of the business," said Hank Stram, head coach of the New Orleans Saints. Stram, it should be noted, was the head coach of the Kansas City Chiefs for a decade, during which he achieved the reputation of assembling the largest playbook in the NFL.

You undoubtedly remember the "Offense of the Seventies" with which Stram's Chiefs won Super Bowl IV. It was a multiple offense, replete with formations, almost infinite variations on each formation, "trick" plays such as reverses and halfback-option passes, and the like. The offense of the seventies lasted one season. It was torn apart by the defenses of the forties . . . the same defenses that were once used to stop single-wing attacks.

In any case, Stram has proved over the years that he knows as many formations as anybody. He has also exhibited no reluctance whatsoever to use everything he knows. Therefore, his style of coaching demands more intelligent players, right?

"Whatever it is that Hank does with us," said center John Hill during the 1976 season, "it all boils down to a few plays that start off differently. There is nothing confusing about a Stram offense. He's still cutting and shaping it to meet the kind of personnel he has to play."

But we digress. The playbook is the issue. And it usually contains far more information than plays and instructional diagrams. There is, for instance, a section of rules and regulations generally headed: "Team Policy." It will include a schedule of fines—late for meeting, missing a bus, missing a practice, missing an airplane, regulations concerning dress code (if any), curfew, press relations (if any), general instructions on how to wear the equipment, how to use the machinery, where to find the trainer, how to report medical insurance claims, and a raft of addenda.

In it will also be found general statements about last season's success—or lack of it. Frequency charts will be included—"last season we had an average of sixty-seven plays on offense, thirty-nine of which were running plays, twenty-seven of which were run to the right"—and so on. There will also be many blank pages on which the players will make notes, draw diagrams, jot down cogent points of interest ("I miss my mommy"), file away questions to ask the unit coach, and so on.

Then the playbook becomes more specific. What may follow next is an "offensive system" of basic diagrams, general terminology (hole numbers, position codes), the huddle structure, quarterback calls and signals, various cadences for the calling of such signals. And more diagrams. And still more and more and more diagrams. For instance: "Our basic off-tackle play is called Slant Thirty-four. This designation is arrived at because the three-back will run a slant at the four-hole. It is normally run out of a brown (or Blue or Red or Green) formation. This play represented 47 percent of our running game last year, and with it we gained an average of 3.2 yards per carry."

The numbering of the holes—which in effect is the numbering of the offensive linemen and/or the gaps they are expected to create—is another basic piece of information. Generally, most pro teams are numbered odd-right, even left. This means the one-hole belongs to the center-going-right; the three-hole is the right guard; the five-hole is the right tackle; the seven-hole is one of the on-the-line receivers, normally the tight end; and the nine-hole (which many teams do not designate) is the area that must be cleared on a sweep to the right. On the other half of the line, the 0-hole is the center-going-left; the two-hole is the left guard; the four-hole is the left tackle; the six- and eight-holes belong to an on-the-line receiver and the area to be cleared for a sweep to the left.

In a pro set, which means two obvious running backs, the halfback may be called the two-back and the fullback the three-back. There are letters, not numbers, for the receivers. They are X, Y, and Z. The tight end is Y. The flanker (back off the line of scrimmage) is Z. The split end is X.

Ready?

"Slant thirty-four, Y-right, on four."

What does that mean? The play just called will send the fullback (the three-back) into the four-hole (left tackle) on a cadence call of four. The tight end (Y) is going to line up on the right, away from the play, in an attempt to influence the defense into covering him.

Fine. Easily understood and quickly grasped, right? Okay. But some teams do their numbering backward, which means a Slant-thirty-four translates into the halfback running to the right tackle hole. Or some teams will number the line holes the same but number the backs differently. Or the backs will be numbered the same but the line holes will be different.

And when the traded player boils it all down, he realizes the play is the same, only the language has undergone a meaningless flip-flop. "When I first came to the Giants," quarterback Fran Tarkenton remembered, "I'd find myself calling a Viking play every once in a while in the huddle. I'd use the Viking numbering system and the Viking play-theory and I'd say something like 'Y Twenty-nine.' And you know what? Half the time the guys would nod their heads and break the huddle and line up and I wouldn't have the faintest idea of what to do. So I improvised. Usually it worked."

Numbers are fine and numbers are easy, but when the head coach really gets down to some creative labeling, he can make an offense sound like the Tower of Babel. We have been treated to terminology such as Blast and Banana and Bang and Bam and Wham and Crash and Belly and Peel and Tango and on and on. One can imagine a traded player approaching the offensive backfield coach, fixing him with a malevolent stare, and inquiring: "Is the Wham here like the Bam I learned there? Or is your Wham more like the Slam-Crash I learned in Buffalo? Or can I run your Peel the way I used to run the Banana?" For this he went to college?

Next up in our playbook is the defensive section. It, too, begins with certain basic thoughts. George Allen of the Washington Redskins has one formula. He exhorts his defense to do the following things:

1. Hold opponent within fifteen-yard line.
2. Hold opponent to less than three yards [per play, one must assume.]
3. Force three fumbles [again, per game].
4. Make five big plays [ditto].
5. Register three sacks.
6. Allow no run to be longer than twenty-five yards.
7. Allow no long touchdown passes ["long" seems destined to go undefined].
8. Intercept two passes.
9. Stop all third-and-three, third-and-four plays.
10. Allow no more than seventeen points per game.

Furthermore, George offers the four major goals of any defense: Prevent the score; get the ball; gain vertical advantage (field position); score!

The obvious assumption is that a defense that

complies with all of these rules will lead its team to victory every week. Naturally, all these things are impossible, for offenses are given strong counter-suggestions. But Allen's major point comes a bit later in his book. There are, he claims, five ways in which the defense can score. There are only three ways for the offense to score. "A defense," he writes, "can score on a blocked punt, a fumble recovery, a pass interception, a safety, and a punt return. An offense can score only by a run, a pass, or a field goal. Therefore, defenses must be more vital in the team's overall victory. The potential for scoring is greater."

With the players thus armed, the playbook's defensive section continues with philosophies. Blitzing Theories . . . Pass Coverage . . . Run Coverage . . . Zone Versus Man-to-Man Coverage . . . various defensive formations used, others not as frequently used but available nonetheless. As in the offensive section, there will be found the basic diagrams of plays and any number of blank pages that the player either fills in with his responsibilities or simply makes note of his primary and secondary obligations. The playbook is carried all season. It is to be studied and added to, reviewed and referred to, memorized and harkened to. In it, the player will find the coach's total football philosophy.

In effect, the playbook is the textbook. Tests are often administered—orally or written. It becomes a sort of cross-indexed reference file—"when we played St. Louis the last time, they stopped our Slam-Bang-Banana. Why?" So he'll go back to the Slam-Bang-Banana page and relearn the mechanics, if only to make sure he is not the one singled out for blame later on.

The logical consequence of the playbook is the game plan.

Sorry . . . Make that THE GAME PLAN. Upper case and bold. Perhaps surrounded by inspirational pen-and-ink sketches. For coaches make the game plan sound equally as important and awesome as the Holy Grail. They are constantly in search of the pure game plan. They are all self-imagined captains of the *Argo*, adrift over uncharted seas, on an obsessive quest for the Golden Fleece.

Why? What is a game plan? How is it prepared?

First of all, the game plan is perhaps the most over-rated, over publicized bit of nonsense in the world of professional football. Theoretically, it is a list of plays with which a team is sent out to do battle. It is the completion of an enormous amount of work, a chore that has involved scouting reports, film study, computer input and read-outs, meetings with the quarterbacks, off-the-record conversations with other coaches, and whatever form of "edge-seeking" might have been possible. What it boils down to is a "ready list" of plays for the offense and a similar chart of formations and maneuvers for the defense.

And why are game plans overrated and nonsensical? For two very valid reasons. One, they are classic examples of overstated fundamentals. Two, they are almost never followed.

Let us assume the Rams are preparing for a game. Their offense, let us further assume, is strongly influenced by running plays. This is because they have outstanding running backs, along with less than satisfactory quarterbacking. And of all the running plays in their portfolio, their best and most successful is a power sweep. The game plan will show a strong preference for this. But is this because the opponent coming up is weak and vulnerable against the sweep? It is not. It is simply because the power sweep is the

Rams' strongest running play. It always works, or almost always works, and there is no reason not to employ it this week as last week as next week as next month.

Thus all the work and concentration on the enemy's weaknesses is valueless in this instance, since the Rams' coaching staff knew full well the power sweep would be used. Against anyone. So the power sweep will be one of the plays on the ready list—the game plan—every week, the opponent notwithstanding.

There are seldom many plays on the game plan ready list, perhaps ten running plays and half a dozen pass patterns. But the inherent flaw in all game plans is that they are devised and designed while the score is still 0-0. Furthermore, they are calculated to be used from the vantage point of a lead. When the other team takes a lead, especially early in the game, this hallowed game plan often goes out the window. Then it's strictly catch-up football, which involves an altogether different set of plans, many more passes than runs, and forces the offense to attempt to score quickly, tie the score, get ahead, then go back to the game plan.

Really, the offensive portion of a game plan responds to the other team's defensive "frequencies." If, for instance, a defense had been faced with a dozen third-and-four (or less) situations the previous week, and if last week's offense had converted eight times on a draw or a trap off right guard or that old standby, the off-tackle slant, then those plays will be offered as part of this week's game plan.

Game plans are totally dependent, as are all other efforts and attempts in pro football, upon the execution of the play itself. Even if the computer has determined that on second-and-eight a sideline out-pass to the tight end will work, that play must be properly executed. The blocking and the dropback, the pattern and the pass, the misdirection and influence moves must all be right or the play will fail. Computer notwithstanding. Game plan notwithstanding.

"All damned week," Y. A. Tittle used to complain, "we'd practice running plays. Over and over. Dive here . . . sweep there . . . trap and draw and the rest of them. All damned week. Then we'd get into the game on Sunday and when something went wrong we'd go back to the passing."

It should be noted that Tittle was an absolute fanatic when passing was involved. Like most craftsmen, and especially like most gifted, pure passers, he viewed the run as a less attractive alternative. "I can get us there a lot quicker by throwing the ball," he used to say, "and if we have to get there [the end zone], we damned well won't make it by running the ball anyway."

In Tittle's first year with the Giants—it was 1961—there was a bit of tension at first because of the abrupt benching of one of the team's all-time heroes, Charley Conerly. Many of the players, as well as the older segment of the traveling press, resented this apparently callous ending to what had been a glorious career.

Early in the season, the Giants were playing an important game with the Philadelphia Eagles. Both teams were in the running for the Eastern Conference Championship (see how long ago that was?) and it was what the newspaper boys like to call a "must game for both teams."

Tittle took a merciless pounding in the first half. A safety named Don Burroughs was particularly effective, executing blitz after blitz and usually winding up with Tittle's helmet in his hands. For a time, it appeared as if Tittle and Burroughs were Siamese twins or had been fused together in some freak and fiery welding accident.

So Allie Sherman sent in Conerly, and the tide, as newsboys are also fond of saying, turned. Charley passed the Eagles right into runner-up status and sent the Giants toward a conference championship. Tittle was livid after the game. "I didn't have any automatics, any audibles," he protested. "They weren't in the game plan."

How, then, did Conerly manage to stave off the far-ranging Mister Burroughs? "He used the automatics the Giants already had," Tittle said. "It was just from memory. There weren't any in the game plan and I haven't been here long enough to know them."

The game plan, then, is a distillation of what will be found in the playbook. It is a studied approach to victory, combining the best elements of science, scouting, and common sense.

The hell it is.

The playbook is a coach's answer to the charge that he is no different than any other coach.

The game plan, unfortunately, confirms the charge.

7. Every Night at the Movies

The head coach's daughter was married on Saturday. On Sunday a sportswriter asked how the wedding went. "I don't know," said the head coach. "I haven't seen the films yet."

"My wife kept asking me why we never went to the movies," said Alex Webster, who was the head coach of the Giants for five seasons. "I told her I saw so many damned films all week I'd probably bring a pad and pencil and do a chart on Redford's moves."

"Lombardi used to make game film watching traumatic," said Steve Wright, a free-spirit offensive tackle. "On Tuesdays we'd watch Sunday's game . . . and when Vince spotted a mistake, he'd run the thing back and forth . . . back and forth . . . and all the guys would giggle except the one poor bastard who kept missing the same block. Then Lombardi would start screaming about how nothing we ever do can be hidden. I got so paranoid that I'd keep looking over my shoulder when I went to pee."

"Why don't they show us dirty movies? Then, at least, we'd learn something. Not much, but something."
　　　　　—The late Phil King

Paul Brown is generally credited with the inclusion of film study as part of the overall pro football coaching/teaching experience.

Well, maybe.

Brown created, founded, and coached the Cleveland Browns. He even loaned his name to the team for its nickname. One wonders what the NFL would have been like had he been born Paul Schwartz. Or Hassenpfeffer. Anyway, Brown may have been the first to realize the full import of the technical advantages of film study, but it was Wellington Mara, the president of the Giants, who first introduced game films as a part of the coaching technique.

It was 1936, when little Well was a twenty-year-old boy whiz whose father, Timothy, owned the football team. That Christmas, Well's parents gave him a movie camera. "We had tried to get game films a few years earlier," Mara recalled, "but their quality was so poor and their organization so confused that the coaches gave up on the idea. But I knew all our plays . . . and that enabled me to follow the ball because I knew where it was going and who was going to have it. Once the coach [Steve Owen] saw my films, he began to use them as a working tool." (Nobody ever accused Steve Owen of being stupid. If the boss's son had given him a divining rod as a coaching tool, he would have used that, too.)

So it was Wellington Mara, and then George Halas, Clark Shaughnessy, and Paul Brown, who followed suit. And then it was all of the coaches and all of the teams, until today most NFL clubs have a special assistant whose job it is to analyze and break down films into offensive reels, defensive reels, kicking reels, coaching reels, training reels, and highlight reels. They even assemble reels devoted to one player. And as usual, pro football folks have overdone what might have started out as a helpful aid. The word one hears most around these insular men is *film*.

Most players, having never grown accustomed to much studying, need no intensive training program. No film clip is going to grant courage or speed or dedication. "I never paid much attention to my coaches," said the late Phil King, a highly successful fullback with the Giants. "I didn't bother them and they didn't bother me, and when game day came around I went out there and took my licks and gave a few and that was football. All this studying and film-watching is bullshit. Hey, the coach couldn't run for me and I sure as hell didn't want to coach for him. It was a nice arrangement. When they started to show films, I napped."

Steve Wright, who played tackle for the Packers, Bears, Giants, Cardinals, and Redskins, not to mention the Chicago Fire in the ill-fated World Football League, had a similar distaste for coaches, films, and study habits. "I played at Alabama for The Legend [Bear Bryant]," he said. "I didn't like Bear and he sure as hell didn't like me. I refused to kiss his shoes or hum The Lord's Prayer when he walked into the room. So he tried to break me. He put me on the fifth string and I didn't play at all. Then one day he got a call from a Green Bay scout who said the Packers were going to draft me. So Bear started me. 'I'll be damned if I let the pros make a starter out of somebody on my fifth team,' he said.

"Well, I didn't change my ways or my style," Wright continued, "but ol' Bear just didn't want to be embarrassed. Hey, I didn't change in the pros, either. Lombardi couldn't stand me, because he couldn't figure me out. He thought players should never laugh or have fun, because he didn't. He once told me that if they ever had an all-pro award for Idiot Tackle, I'd make the Hall of Fame. But every time he yelled at me I'd laugh in his face, and he got all red and he started to sputter and then he just walked away. You might say I was never surprised when I got traded."

Jimmy Orr was a marvelous wide receiver for the Pittsburgh Steelers and Baltimore Colts. His appreciation of game films knew no bounds—they gave him time to doze.

When the Colts were preparing for Super Bowl III, the game in which the old American League proved it had at least one good quarterback and one good fullback, Jimmy was asked what he knew about cornerback Randy Beverly, one of the Jets' least inspiring starters. Lounging in the sand on a Fort Lauderdale, Florida, beach, Orr smiled. "Well, I just don't know a hell of a lot about him," he drawled. "Every time they put films on the wall, I take a nap. I figure if Beverly—is that his name?—stays with me, I won't be able to catch many passes. But I don't figure he can stay with me, either."

In a way, Orr was right.

He was to be the final Colt in a complicated "fleaflicker" pass play called by quarterback Earl Morrall. Morrall handed off to running back Tom Matte, who started to sprint toward the left side of the line. Suddenly he pulled up and passed the ball back to Morrall, who was to throw to Orr, all alone in the end zone. Damned if it didn't work.

The Jets reacted to Matte's threatened sweep, and Orr nonchalantly loped downfield and suddenly he sprinted away from Beverly, and there he was. Alone. Isolated. Waving his arms and hopping up and down with joy and anticipation. But Morrall forgot where Orr was supposed to be, so he tried to throw over the middle at the goal line to fullback Jerry Hill, and the ball bounced off Hill's shoulder pads into the arms of safety Jim Hudson. Randy Beverly had been beaten by fifteen yards. That play must have been a real thriller on the game films.

Primarily, there are two uses for game films—coaching and scouting. The coaching aspect takes on a cruel edge, because it can be destructive to the egos of the more sensitive players. For this is coaching designed to improve a player through negativism.

"Mostly, the films are viewed to scout your opponent and to grade your players," said Bart Starr, head coach of the Packers. "But you find yourself paying more attention to the players who come out with the lower grades. We have to decide why he isn't playing well . . . whether he was hurt or outplayed by a much better opponent or just not good enough to remain in the starting lineup. So if a linebacker grades out very high, we'll sort of leave him alone. But if another one has missed assignments and tackles, he gets all the attention. I know it's not really compassionate, but in this business you must get the most out of your athletes or find different athletes to solve a problem spot."

The grading of films takes on all sorts of exotic methodologies and procedures. George Allen has devised a formula that demands from all interior linemen an 85 percent performance. "In other words," he explained, "the lineman on passing plays should make his block 85 percent of the time. Scores much lower than that indicate something is wrong. If the player isn't playing hurt, he's just not good enough to continue playing."

But the standards for interior linemen differ from those for players at other positions. The wide receivers, for instance, are still called upon to block, more so by some teams than others. But they are not especially adept blockers, and so Allen's formula demands that they make their blocks on running plays only 55 percent of the time. The tight end, however, is considered an interior lineman in the Allen system and must perform at the 85 percent level.

The grading of defensive players is even more esoteric. And the most difficult players to grade are the deep backs. "Most of our secondary grades are awarded for positioning," Allen said. "How close [a defender] allows a receiver to get to him, for instance, is important. But playing the receiver too loosely isn't good, either, because it becomes impossible to break up a pass. His position on the receiver for certain patterns counts heavily. Did he allow the man to get to his inside or to his outside? This becomes more critical when we see where the receiver wants to go and whether or not the defender made him alter his course.

"Every time a pass is completed, somebody is at fault. A mistake has been made, because in pure terms, perfect defense will never allow a completed pass."

On the other hand, perfect offense demands that a pass never fall incomplete. What we have here is a philosophical conflict.

Vince Costello was a wondrously effective linebacker, mostly for the Cleveland Browns. Now an assistant coach with a bright future, he still carries some strange ideas about defense.

"Every time the offense gains even an inch, somebody on the defense has made an error," he insists. "If the defense has been properly assembled, and if the defensive players are competent and have been properly prepared, no offensive play should gain even that inch. Of course, you never get a perfect defensive game, but you should be able to compensate for your 'errors' by stopping them for a loss on the play after they made an advance.

"I don't care how well the defense plays. If it's third-and-ten and the offense gains even a yard, it wasn't a perfect defensive reaction. Of course, I'd rather they gained that yard than ten of them for a first down. But you have to set impossibly high standards for your players. If you don't, they'll get too satisfied with themselves and that can explode a game."

Allen exhorts his players to "never be fooled by the play-action passes." That is, indeed, far easier to say than to do, because from the other side of the field, offenses have been designed to fool defenses, and the play-action pass is perhaps the most difficult maneuver to sniff out in time. Which is where films can help.

Let's use Fran Tarkenton, the all-time leading passer in NFL history, as an example. Little Francis, who made the scramble a romantic and electrifying play, loves the play-action fake more than anything. He also loves to throw to his backs, since he recognizes the limitations of his rather weak arm.

Well, any team preparing to play the Minnesota Vikings has seen films of Tarkenton's last three games. At least. And the defense has witnessed his deceptive style of using play-action passes. So when he starts to hand the ball off to a running back, the defense isn't going to honor it, right? Wrong. What happens is that everybody on the defense smiles smugly, says "he ain't really gonna give the ball to Foreman," and drops off to wait for the pass. And, indeed, Francis does give the ball to Foreman, who finds little or no resistance from the stunned defenders.

"The play-action pass, especially when it's used to get a ball to a running back, is impossible to defend," insists Tarkenton, "especially if you have as gifted a back as Chuck Foreman. If you get the ball to him in the secondary, he'll never be tackled by the first man who tries. It's a guaranteed gain. But if they overload one side, looking for Foreman to get a pass, or if they play back off Foreman, they are leaving themselves vulnerable somewhere else. It's my job to find the areas of compensation and exploit them. The worst kind of quarterback, no matter how much talent he may have, is the kind who can't change his mind. Being too rigid mentally can only hurt a team."

There are, however, several dangers inherent in viewing game films, all of them creations of the coaches who grow far too dependent on the celluloid crutch. "It is entirely possible to out-think yourself," admits John McVay, who became head coach of the Giants in 1976, after Bill Arnsparger was dismissed at midseason. "There is a very real danger. It could happen like this: Say you are going to play the Redskins in the thirteenth game of the season. It's the second game against them, and the first one was opening day. Now that's three months or so, and no team in this game stays the same over that long a period of time.

"Well, in that first game, they might have been into sweeps. And the sweeps might have worked well. Now, in three months' time, maybe their best runner has been injured, or has burned himself out, or maybe their best pulling guard is on the sidelines. Something. Anything. Or maybe the coaches simply changed up and decided slants and power drives would work better late in the season.

"If you put too much effort into [learning] those sweeps, you'll find out that you wasted a lot of time and it didn't matter. And since there is only a certain amount of days in which to prepare a defense, you might well pass up critical preparation in order to get ready for something they won't use anymore.

"There's another risk, too. In this business, there is

a certain amount of poker-playing. So, let's assume you have a big game coming up with Washington, a game that might decide the championship in your division. And say the week before they had the chance to play some weaker team that didn't require much in the way of special preparation.

"So they go with the most basic of all game plans. They play a standard four-three defense and they use only the most rudimentary of offenses, and you watch that film and think, 'Damn, this is a piece of cake.' Then you get out on the field and suddenly they're like snakes let out of a box, going every which way with weird plays and odd defenses and abnormal coverages and where are you then? You're dead, that's where you are.

"What happened was that coach decided to show you an 'artificial' game. He didn't want to give you any real clues, so he took the chance that he could win that game without bringing in any of the special things he had ready for you. And if you're not careful, you'll get trapped. That's probably the strongest reason for scouting games in person and not relying totally on film. You could wind up studying outdated or intentionally misleading films, and when there are only fourteen games in a season, you can't afford to be caught even once. You don't get paid for being stupid, or even careless."

A classic example of intentional subterfuge occurred in 1969, when the New York Jets, then defending Super Bowl champions, had an immensely important home game with the Kansas City Chiefs (who would inherit the Super Bowl mantle). The Chiefs had one of the finest wide receivers of all time, Otis Taylor. He was big and strong (six-three, 210) and he ran with the speed of a sprinter (indeed, he was once clocked in

9.9 for the 100-yard dash). Kansas City head coach Hank Stram, who earned a well-deserved reputation for assembling the thickest playbook in football, used Otis in a multitude of ways.

But when the game began, none of these were different from what the Jets expected. Otis flanked out wide, and Otis went into motion, and Otis closed up and pretended to be a tight end. But the Jets were prepared for these eventualities. They had him covered.

By late in the game the Jets were losing, but not by a lot, and it was still anybody's Sunday. Otis came out as a setback. He lined up as a halfback about five yards to the right of and behind quarterback Lenny Dawson. He didn't go into motion. He didn't reset himself as a wide receiver, flanker, or tight end. He stayed put as the cadence was being called.

The Jets didn't know who should cover him, who should knock him off-balance, or whether to deal with him as a blocker. And Otis simply took off from that spot—untouched—and sped deep into the secondary. Dawson, after wheeling and faking a handoff, straightened up and threw as far as he could. Otis was there—all alone—to haul in the touchdown pass and turn a tight game into an ultimate 34-16 rout.

The two teams met again at the end of the season in a playoff game at Shea Stadium. Kansas City won, 13-6, with a last-minute, nail-biting goal line stand. But that game would not have taken place if Stram and Dawson hadn't fooled the Jets earlier in the season. "We had that play in our offense all season," Stram crowed afterward, "but we never used it until now. I think it was the right time for it, don't you?"

Stram scored again in the Super Bowl with unexpected, unorthodox, and, most important, unfilmed plays. The other wide receiver, Frank Pitts, had never run an end-around. Their Super Bowl IV opponents, the Minnesota Vikings, knew that. Not once in any of the game films shown had Pitts done anything unusual. So in the Super Bowl, which is a hell of a time to experiment, Stram sent in reverses for Pitts twice, and these resulted in long gains that helped to crack the game wide open.

"Of course we have defenses for reverses," said the Vikings' coach, Bud Grant, during a post-mortem interview, "but we never expected them to use any. They hadn't done so all season."

Defensive specialists like Arnsparger, however, would insist that any sound defense should have built-in "support patterns" to take care of unexpected plays. Clearly, the saying is far simpler than the doing. Arnsparger's defenses fared better than most (both in Miami and with the Giants) against the unexpected, but there is never a guaranteed approach to eliminating the sudden, game-breaking surprise. Even studying films can't do it.

But "teams that have to resort to surprise plays," said the late Vince Lombardi, "are hiding a weakness or admitting that you have the better team and they must use trickery to win."

Perhaps. But surprise plays do work, especially in games between evenly matched teams, and there is absolutely no way of preventing their success without luck being a strong factor.

The actual viewing of game films has become a science, too. And it has served to separate defensive players and offensive players into isolated units. "I don't have the faintest idea what sort of offense the Giants play," said quarterback Steve Ramsey, on the day in March of 1977 that he was traded by the Broncos to the Giants. "We played them last season, sure, but all I watched was their defensive films. Hell of a defense, too. Gave us a bad time all day. So I guess I'll be at my best in scrimmages, because I really studied that defense. But it will be like starting all over when I try to learn their offense."

Defensive players watch offense films. Offensive players watch defense films. Exclusively.

As a result, when you ask a middle linebacker his opinion as to the best in the league at his position, he's at a loss. He doesn't see linebackers nearly as often as fans and sportswriters. "Go ask the quarterback," said Minnesota's Jeff Siemon to one such query, "I don't have the faintest idea."

. There is, of course, a reason for all this. The coaches demand that their players put forth full concentration every working day of the season. Of what use would it be to the middle linebacker to watch defenses? He is not concerned with beating them; his only concern is with stopping offenses. And if the middle linebacker needs to learn more about his own position, he has his coach instead, to whom he can go with questions or suggestions.

Naturally, every coach in the league is capable of teaching his man how to play like Dick Butkus. Isn't he?

"By the time we get through summer camp, there just isn't much more time for basic instruction," said Buddy Parker, who had a long, often successful, and always colorful career as head coach of the Detroit Lions and Pittsburgh Steelers in the 1950s and 1960s. "When the season starts, it's a game every week and practice almost every day, and if the players don't know how to play their positions by then, either they won't be on the team or the coach has made a terrible mistake."

Parker, all during his years as a coach, constantly endeared himself to the sportswriters on the beat. At one end-of-season banquet, he was asked about his plans for a quarterback for the following season. "Well," drawled the man from deep in the heart of Texas, "I got three kids who look pretty good and [veteran] Ed Brown. If all else fails, I'll go with that fucking Brown."

Parker also made sure not to endear himself to one of the NFL's top fullbacks of the early sixties, John Henry Johnson. For the week leading up to a critical match with the Giants in 1961, Parker insisted he was going to bench his star for his casual blocking. No one really believed he would do it. Then again, no one really understood just how sincere Buddy Parker was.

The morning of the game, a cluster of visiting press descended on the Steeler dressing room (that was another departure from the norm tolerated by Parker: pre-game visitations). "Coach, are you really going to keep John Henry out of the game?" inquired one of the visiting pencils.

"Yep."

"But why, coach? He's your only good runner."

"Yep, but that lazy sucker ain't blockin' worth a shit, and if he don't block, he don't play."

What made this all the more startling is that Johnson was standing next to Parker when he made his statement. And Johnson didn't play. And the Steelers didn't win. But Buddy Parker had established himself as a straight talker. Johnson improved his blocking techniques dramatically the following week.

Parker, the only man who ever challenged the legendary Bobby Layne to a drinking contest and got turned down, also had a unique relationship with God. His wife, the morning of another game with the Giants (a team Parker almost never beat), overheard him praying in the small chapel he had installed in their know the only really important thing is that no one home in Pittsburgh.

Roughly, he said the following: "God, I know this is just a game, and I know you don't choose sides, and I gets hurt. But tell me, God, why did you give all the great receivers to those damned Giants?"

Buddy didn't much care about films. "I know what we can do," he said, "and if we find a team that can't stop us, we'll probably win. But most teams are better than we are [in Pittsburgh], so driving myself crazy staring at films ain't gonna make much difference, is it?" Most other coaches, however, have made the study of films an obsession. To paraphrase Karl Marx, "Game films are the opiate of the coaches."

"Before I had even agreed to sign with the Giants," recalled fullback Larry Csonka, "coach [Bill] Arnsparger had me in a dark room, watching films." Ah, yes, good old Bill Arnsparger. If ever a man had an obsession with watching films, it was this former and present defensive whiz of the Miami Dolphins, who took thirty months out of his life as a successful assistant coach to be hired and then fired as head coach of the Giants.

Stories about Bill and his films are legendary on the pro football beat. In Miami, as the Dolphins built their No-Name Defense into successive Super Bowl championships, he acquired the nickname "One More Reel." "The man was constantly studying films," said one of the Dolphins' running backs of those years, Jim Kiick. "When you thought he was finished . . . after seven, eight hours of watching . . . you'd hear one of the coaches go in and ask if he wanted dinner. 'Oh, sure,' Bill would say, 'but I just want to see one more reel.' "

And when he was fired by the Giants, who had nothing to show for their game filming except horror movies, he was hired in three days to return to the Dolphins and his friend Don Shula. "He came down right away," remembered a Miami sportswriter, "and left his family back in New York to sell the house. He took a motel room right near the practice field . . . a bare, spare motel that didn't even have a coffee shop. I asked him about it once, asked why he didn't find anything more comfortable.

" 'Hell, I don't need much,' he said. 'I stay in the fieldhouse until ten, eleven at night, and the room has everything I need. A bed, a table for the projector, and an electric outlet to plug in the projector.' "

Such dedication demands its reward; if not a Coach of the Year plaque, then certainly an Oscar for film editing.

There are, uncontestably, values to be gained from film study. But the abuse of films, or their overuse, or a total reliance on them serves no real purpose other than to produce fatigue, promote tedium, and ensure the incomes of optometrists.

"I always studied films to see the movements of the defensive backs," said Raymond Berry, one of the NFL's all-time outstanding receivers. "You'd be amazed at how much a film will tell you, if you know what to look for and how to exploit it. Some backs had their own trademarks . . . little things they did, things I'm sure they weren't even conscious of . . . like always beginning their back-pedal on the same foot, or crossing their legs for just a fraction of an instant, or always going up to block a pass with the same hand. If you   knew   these   things,   you   could   compose countermoves. I kept a notebook on every defensive back in the league, and most of the information I put together came out of films."

Berry was also a player who studied other offenses and compiled notebooks on other receivers, both the great and the anonymous.

"Being a receiver means perfecting many different moves and then being able to put together three or four of them, or more, in one pass pattern. The moves you use, and the combinations you choose, are based strictly on the man you're playing against. But finding those moves means having to study other receivers. Some do one thing well, others do several things well, and even a rookie can sometimes show you a move you haven't seen or tried or thought about.

"Of course, the better receivers always have the better moves. I can remember studying men like Lenny Moore and Elroy Hirsch and Del Shofner and Bill Howton and Kyle Rote. And I'm sure I must have borrowed something from each of them."

This dedication produced its own reward. Berry is still looked upon with awe and spoken of in hushed, respectful terms. Almost every defensive player who tried to stop this Man of a Thousand Moves has his own "favorite" catch to remember.

"I don't think I ever saw him drop a ball," said Hall of Famer, Night Train Lane. "But more than that, I saw him catch several passes he had no right to catch, or even get close to. The man was just unreal. You couldn't intimidate him and you couldn't really stay close to him. He didn't have great speed, but I'd rather cover a guy with great speed and not many moves. It was maddening. I'd have him right in my sights and suddenly he'd be free and clear and I'd never know how he did it."

Coaches also display a tendency to show rookies film clips of superstars at the same positions—a so-called "training aid." But it remains a mystery as to what benefits a rookie can derive from studying the way O. J. Simpson conducts himself in the broken field. There are few, if any, runners with the same abilities, and for the mediocre journeyman running back, such viewing can produce depression and a loss of confidence rather than provide helpful hints. Coaches will protest this last. "It's the moves we want them to see. It's how the great ones do things we want our kids to see."

Sure. And what made Deacon Jones a great defensive end were his moves, but if everyone were capable of executing these moves. Deacon would have had a lot of company at the top.

In addition to analyzing their opponents and judging the performance of their own players, NFL teams are devout in their worship of celluloid when it comes to evaluating draftable college seniors. Rarely does a team make a selection—any selection, no matter what the round—without having seen the prospective draft choice on film.

"We break down college films a bit differently," said Peter Hadhazy, general manager of the Cleveland Browns. "Obviously, we're not terribly concerned with who won or lost the game, and why. We want to see the specific player as much as possible and in as many different situations as possible. So we chart his game, no matter what his position, and determine how well he performed his function on each and every play.

"There is much more to it, also. We want to see his footwork, his blocking style, his overall speed, his quickness. We want to see how quickly he gets off the ball . . . into his man . . . how he avoids tacklers . . .

blockers . . . what sort of patterns he runs . . . how long he needs to develop his pattern.

"What we do, actually, is dissect his game, every practical aspect of it, and then judge his performance against others. Sure, size is important. Or speed. Or strength. But you can find a pot-full of big, fast, and strong college seniors who simply can't play football. This is another way of eliminating a mistake."

Another factor enters into this sort of film study—the level of competition faced by the prospective draftee. When Cincinnati drafted quarterback Ken Anderson, for instance, there was little opportunity to see how he fared against equal or superior opposition. Anderson played at tiny Augustana (Illinois) College, hardly a bellwether school in big-time football. "There are two factors to consider when the kid is playing at a small school," Hadhazy continued. "First, you run the risk of overestimating him. Second, you run the risk of underestimating him.

"Let me explain that. If a kid is very, very good, especially at a position like quarterback, he is going to be clearly superior to the other quarterbacks in his conference or competition circle. So everything he does will look brilliant. You have to be sure he would continue to look that good when he is thrust into a high-level situation.

"But because he's so clearly superior, you can forget that his teammates aren't capable of providing him with the accompanying support. He may overthrow or underthrow his receivers, for example, but are you sure it's his fault and not because the receivers simply aren't capable of playing up to his standards. I mean, if the kid throws a perfect fifteen-yard square-out pass, and it falls incomplete, did he throw it too soon or too long or was his receiver unable to run that pattern?

"What you try to do with a player from a very small school is isolate him, watch his mechanics, his style, his moves. Then you compare those notes against the pro players, or you try to take a quarterback from Tiny University and transplant him—in your mind—onto the squad of Giant University. Or compare him with a blue-chip quarterback from a major school, preferably a team with a high-powered passing offense. Does Smith from the small school do things as well as Jones from the major school?

"If he can compare favorably, he might even be a better selection, because the small schools generally have less available coaches on the staff and the kid probably didn't get all the help he could have used. The kid at the major school did, and if he's no better than the other quarterback, the one without the intense training, perhaps he won't continue to develop and will wind up not as good after the same three-four years in the NFL."

Coaches normally don't have the time during the season to view film of college prospects, which puts that burden on the scouts. Therefore, teams are more likely to hire as a scout a former coach or player since such a man will have had the experience of film-analyzing.

"Sometimes, you see things on film you can't possibly notice during the game," said Jerry Shay, the Giants' chief scout. "The games are played too fast to really zero in on one player. Especially when we're looking at a possible first-round kid, film is critical. Is the big lineman making his blocks because he's so much bigger than the opponent, or is he doing it properly? It gets so involved with a first-round pick that you want to see everything, and most times you're sure you missed something."

On less frequent occasions, a scout may see something on film that was totally unnoticed during the game, and several pro players owe their careers to a scout's keen eye in a darkened room, catching something he failed to see in the stands or the press box during the playing of the game.

There is another facet of films in pro football. Its name is NFL Films, Inc. First of all, this corporate division of the NFL shoots live, color film of every game played by every team in the league—exhibition, regular season, playoff, as well as the Super Bowl. Even the Pro Bowl, that great, unwanted entity which serves as an anticlimax to the Super Bowl, is preserved on celluloid by the NFL Films people. Why?

It would appear the answer is: Why not? NFL Films makes a good deal of money.

Each team purchases its own annual Highlights film from NFL Films, Inc., and for many clubs it is the only time during the season that something good shows up on the screen. Highlight films are for use by fan clubs, church groups, fund-raising bodies, and the like—at no cost. The films are also shown by those players who serve on a team's speaking bureau, and each team has one of these. The Highlight films are sponsored by a local business or community organization, so the team even gets its money back, and their advertising value is limitless.

NFL Films, Inc., also produces hundreds of feature films for public consumption, sells some of them to airlines, sells others to various other commercial groups, and has entered into an agreement with Pro Sports Entertainment, Inc., for the year-long syndication of three different series—NFL Game of the Week, This Is the NFL, and NFL: Great Teams, Great Years. This is a worthwhile money-maker, for it will put the NFL into time slots it has never been—off-season weekend air-ing, off-season prime-time airing, in-season weekday airing.

It can be reasonably estimated that NFL Films, Inc., spends more than a million dollars each year in the shooting and processing of its Highlights films. These are not the familiar coaching films, which are in black-and-white and often grainy, but professionally pro-duced entertainment films, complete with sound track. Usually someone in the world of broadcasting closely allied with the NFL is chosen to narrate these High-light films—Frank Gifford, Pat Summerall, Paul Hornung, etc. Not so for the NFL Films features, in which dramatic talent rather than NFL identity is sought. Some NFL films use George C. Scott as narra-tor, which takes them somewhat beyond the scope of a game.

And NFL Properties, Inc., zealously protects its patents and copyrights. just as NFL Films, Inc., closely guards its strips of celluloid. Bob Hayes, who was once the finest, fastest, and most famous of all NFL re-ceivers, opened a men's clothing store in Dallas during the height of his career. On the facade of the building, he had painted the emblem of the Dallas Cowboys' helmet. He was threatened with a lawsuit by NFL Properties if he didn't take it down or pay—exorbi-tantly—for the right to use it.

That's how NFL Films and NFL Properties operate. They sell what they can and they guard what they cannot sell. Those occasional "comedy" films of NFL game foolishness that are seen on "The Tonight Show" are paid for by the network. Nothing goes for nothing.

To independent film producers packaging thirty-minute shows on football for television, this has often served as an insurmountable obstacle in acquiring quality footage. For example, a special documentary on Vince Lombardi had to be produced with network tape, since the cost of film clips of Lombardi and his Green Bay Packers was prohibitive. Thus, NFL Films, Inc., often stands in the way of deriving magnificent promotional value for the league by its insistence on payment and being properly credited.

A final note about the product put out by NFL films. The soundtrack music they use is overbearing and unnecessarily dramatic. We are not watching the invasion of Poland, the sinking of a Nazi warship, or the birth of a volcano. Just a football game. It is just another indication of the oversaturation of the NFL—a legend in its own mind.

8. The Media, Mostly Newspapers

"I am going to make the newspapermen in pro football obsolete," Bill Arnsparger stated paranoiacally to one of the New York Giants' administrative assistants.

"Then how the hell will the stories of the games get into the papers?" demanded the assistant.

A horde of newspapermen attended the press conference at which the Giants made Arnsparger obsolete.

Television and radio pay for the right to broadcast NFL games. Newspapers pay nothing for the right to cover NFL games. Perhaps if they kick in something, they'll get better treatment from the player and coaches. But then they would probably report only good news, to protect their investment.

With the almost total takeover of the airwaves by the television networks, newspapers are more in demand than ever. Not only do fans like to read about what they *saw* the day before, they also appreciate having what they *heard* the day before translated into English.

Several head coaches in the league insist that the newspapermen talk to them before being allowed to interview the players. George Allen is the leader of this movement.

Bad enough to have such as Billy Kilmer
alternately curse or ignore the press, but why should
I first have to be bored by George?

Players and coaches (and, to a lesser extent, owners
and general managers) variously regard the print
media as useless, conspiratorial, insipid, uneducated,
ill-prepared, disloyal, freeloading, dishonest, irreverent,
and prying.

To some of those descriptions—disloyalty, prying,
irreverent—we must all plead guilty. The overriding
factor is that the teams we cover do not sign our salary
checks. Our newspapers do. Therefore, our loyalty is to
the newspapers. We are assigned to teams by the newspapers, our expenses are paid by the newspapers, and
our work is judged (graded, if you will) by the newspapers.

We are a group the teams must tolerate, for the alternative (no coverage, no free publicity, no drumming
up of fan interest, and resultant ticket purchases) is
not at all attractive, and even the teams realize that.

Before proceeding with the horror stories, there is a
need to defend oneself against the common excla-
mation of:

"Boy, what a glamorous job you have!"

That is usually followed by:

"Do you really travel with the team?"

"Do you really know O. J. Simpson?"

"Do you really get into the games for nothing?"

Frequently, no doubt as a product of my cynicism, I
have failed to recognize the inherent glamour in a trip
such as the following:

Board a chartered jet in New York on Friday afternoon. Sit in the cramped coach-section seats because
the coaches and selected veterans have staked out the

first-class accommodations. Fly to San Diego, being fed en route something that can only be called "Slippery Chicken" stuffed with no-one-wants-to-ask-what. Arrive in San Diego complete with headache, stomach ache, and jet lag. Try to sleep. Awake at 4 A.M. because at home it's time to get up. Kill most of the day reading magazines in the hotel gift shop or trying to talk to lounging athletes. Go to an exhibition game at 8 P.M. (11 P.M. back home). Rush through a story in order to make the team bus (which leaves forty-five minutes after the game) to the airport. Board the chartered jet. Fly all night. Arrive at JFK Airport at 8 A.M. Drive home. Sleep all day.

Glamorous, right?

How about freezing in unheated press boxes in Chicago, in unenclosed press boxes in Washington, or getting drenched in leaky press boxes in St. Louis?

Glamorous, right?

How about spending New Year's Eve and Christmas Eve on the road in near-empty hotels, waiting for playoff games and championship games, and getting dirty looks from waiters when you arrive in the dining room for dinner when they'd rather be home?

How about getting frostbite in Green Bay or pneumonia in Minneapolis?

Glamorous, right?

Glamorous, wrong. Much of the time spent in travel to cover a pro football team is a bloody bore. There is no fury like a woman scorned on New Year's Eve, especially if she is your wife. Once I didn't know when to call my wife to wish her a happy new year, since I was in Los Angeles. Do I call her at 9 P.M. in order to get her at midnight, or do I call her at midnight and risk additional wrath by waking her at 3 A.M. Or do I risk calling at all and getting no answer?

Once I missed New Year's Eve entirely. I was trekking back from Green Bay, which meant flying the airline whose motto might be—"In case of emergency, please kick hole in floor and deplane"—to Chicago, then switching to another airline for New York. The flight from Chicago took off at 11 P.M. Somewhere in the air, midnight arrived. But by the time we landed, it was past midnight in New York. Where was I when the new year dawned? Beats me.

But I do know O. J. Simpson. Whoopee! All this is part of the job. It falls under the heading of Earning A Living. There is far more interest—for me—in the interplay between newspaperman and athlete, newspaperman and coach.

Most athletes and coaches, having readily accepted the mystique of pro football, sincerely believe that the newsmen covering the team are ignorant of the game's nuances, language, and concepts. In the beginning of the pro football boom, that was generally true. The newsmen assigned to cover the NFL teams were either veterans of the major league baseball beat (which used to be a large daily's primary sports assignment), youngsters fresh from college dorms, copy b pressed into service in order to accommodate the gr ng number of readers interested in this professional football business. And they really didn't know a hell of a lot. But they learned, much to the displeasure of the coaches and the players, who no longer had an exclusive hold on the barely sophisticated aspects of the sport.

It is difficult to portray the dismay of a head coach when asked: "Say, coach . . . that sixty-yard touchdown pass you got burned on . . . was it because the free safety didn't rotate to the weakside or because the strong safety didn't force quickly enough or because the weakside linebacker took the play-fake and wasn't there to get in the way of the decoy circle pattern the fullback ran?"

In such instances, the coach would become defensive.

"What do you think, smart-ass?"

And when the newsman answered: "Well, without seeing the films, of course, I'd say it was the strong safety, because he made the same mistake twice in the third quarter and the quarterback finally caught on and exploited it . . . , and he's been burned four other times this season on that same Zig-Deep pattern," the coach knew for sure he had been uncovered.

Today, pro football more than ever, is covered with unique intensity by newspapermen, because we are at war with the TV networks. Therefore, we must bring insights of the sport and recreate scenes not captured by the all-seeing, but badly guided, electronic eye. Many of the pro football correspondents around the country keep voluminous charts during the game and are aware of everything from how many tackles a linebacker registered to how many passes were thrown into the cornerback's area, or when the defense was in a zone, combination-zone, or man-to-man alignment. Some of these charts are supplied by the individual team, which is another reason for keeping our own. Untrained eyes do not produce accurate charts.

As an example, the NFL's statistical arm was never more embarrassed than after Super Bowl IX, when the official team statistics credited the Minnesota Vikings with twenty-two net rushing yards, and Paul Zimmerman of the *New York Post*, perhaps the most fervent chart keeper of them all, discovered the Vikings had gained only eighteen, that a two-yard loss was erroneously marked down as a two-yard gain. It was never documented that a man's job was lost because of that error, but there were such rumors.

The point is this: The newsmen know what is happening, what has happened, and, to a relatively accurate degree, what should happen. This is not good for the mystique. It widens the circle of insiders, and with each new member, the power of the mystique diminishes. In order to keep the newsmen out of the way and in a state of ignorance (television people, except for the ex-players, never stray from this particular state of grace), teams have tried various ways of dispensing non-information.

The Oakland Raiders, for example, do not announce their list of summer camp roster cuts . . . and not even head coaches can instantly determine the identity of a player in a group of sixty to eighty, each wearing a helmet and often duplicate jersey numbers. Al Davis, the Managing General Partner of the Raiders, is highly suspicious of the press. "We only have to tell the league office of our waivers," he once said. "If the press has to know, let them figure it out every day at practice, see who is missing." That might not be impossible, except for the fact that more often than not the Raiders conduct closed practices.

The famous Bill Arnsparger, in his first season as head coach of the Giants, went out of his way to acquire, via trade, a linebacker named Bruce Bannon. He pursuaded Bannon, a highly intelligent chemicals salesman, to leave a solid job and renounce a premature retirement. Bannon had been drafted by the Miami Dolphins when Arnsparger, then as now, was the team's defensive coordinator, and he obviously saw a wide streak of ability in the Penn State graduate. Bannon was reciprocal in his admiration of Arnsparger. "Coach Bill is the only man I'd play for again," he said the day he joined the Giants' summer-camp-in-progress.

And so, on the day of the final cuts that were to achieve the roster total of forty-three, Bannon was cut. He was stunned. The press was surprised. The question was a natural: "Bill, why did you cut Bannon?" The answer was predictable: "Because we had to get down to forty-three."

Oh. And thanks, Bill.

Another Arnsparger story. After an early-season game against Philadelphia that not only ended in defeat but produced injuries to two regular offensive linemen, Bill was asked:

"Coach, with the injuries to Mullen and Hicks, who will play the offensive line next week?"

To which our hero retorted:

"We have eight offensive linemen. Two are hurt. That leaves us with six. Five will play."

Oh.

The point to be made is this: Coaches and players, for the most part, are pleased to dispense bland information to interviewers. But when the interviewer looks too closely at pro football, the coach and athlete suddenly freeze. There is a very real suspicion of newspapermen, which does not carry over to television and radio folks. And there are very good reasons for this, for television and radio interviews are always bland and colorless, have specified time allotments, and bear the limitations of those doing the interviewing.

The daily newspapermen, however, are after, and get, different material. They know more about football than do the TV and radio people. And they need more information about the game each week, i.e., about practices, plans and strategies, and starting lineups. They also have the opportunity to see the players at their worst—in practice and immediately after a game in their locker room. They are, in effect, too close for comfort, and their proximity gives them certain vibrations that result in the asking of "embarrassing" questions, the answers to which require the divulging of "classified" material.

So the daily press is somewhat ostracized. Those who write critically are often ignored, or worse, chastised. A fellow who covers the Los Angeles Rams, and who had been critical of the team's yawn-inducing offense, once decided to call plays from the press box for an entire game. He amused his peers by being right on more than 85 percent of the Rams' calls. As predictable as that offense might have been, he could not have achieved such a high rate of accuracy without knowing the game well.

Several teams close their midweek practices to the daily newspapermen. Others refuse access to the locker rooms during the week. Some instruct their team physicians and trainers to refuse newspapermen's questions. And still others insist that even the harmless "feature-type" interviews be conducted under controlled circumstances, i.e., in a meeting room and by appointment, rather than allowing a casual stroll through the clubhouse.

Fan attendance at practices is frequently forbidden, and in one instance has led to one of pro football's most hilarious anecdotes. It was 1966, and the Giants were training for a week in California prior to a game with the Rams. The Giants were on their way to a 1-12-1 season, a season in which they were to set records for most points allowed and most touchdowns allowed, records that still stand, despite the valiant efforts of the Tampa Bay Buccaneers in 1976.

While training at a local junior college, head coach

Allie Sherman spotted a "spy" looking on. He sent one of the equipment men to chase away the interloper. It didn't work. Then he sent one of the assistant coaches. That didn't work, either. Finally he went himself, approached the man, and demanded that he leave immediately. "This is a secret practice," he barked.

To which the fan responded: "What are you hiding, Sherman, your one-and-eight record?"

And in 1956, when the Giants were preparing to meet the Chicago Bears for the NFL championship, head coach Jim Lee Howell was sure that George Halas, the owner/coach of the Bears, had secreted two spies in one of the apartment buildings overlooking old Yankee Stadium in the South Bronx. So he spent most of the week working with a twelve-man offense, specifically to fool the men he was sure were diagramming each and every formation. "Let them figure out which guy isn't real," was his philosophy. It must have worked. The Giants won that game, 47-7.

Once—only once—did I find myself involved in the nasty practice of keeping information from the public. It was the Friday before the 1962 NFL championship game between the Green Bay Packers and the Giants. The Packers were already in town, and they had just concluded a workout in Yankee Stadium. I was in their locker room, looking for an interview, when I heard the door close.

I was locked in—with the Packers and head coach Vince Lombardi. Since a row of lockers stood between them and me, I wasn't seen. And suddenly, from the other side of the lockers, I heard Lombardi talking with all-pro center Jim Ringo (later head coach of the Buffalo Bills).

"How is the arm?"

"I can't feel it at all, coach," Ringo responded.

"Will you be able to play?" Lombardi wondered.

"You can't keep me off the field," Ringo said, "but I can't feel the arm and I might not be able to block well."

Then they saw me. Lombardi raged. Ringo was more gentle. "Listen," he explained, "if the Giants find out about my arm, they'll all take shots at it, and I might even get a permanent injury. It's some kind of nerve damage, I think. But I plan to play, and I'd appreciate it if you don't write about my injury. I think I can make it if nobody knows I'm hurting. And I'll make this promise. I'll keep it a secret, too, and I won't say anything about it to any of the other newspaper guys. It can be your story after the game, okay?"

I agreed, because I didn't want a man permanently injured because of something I wrote. It wasn't that important. Also, I didn't like the picture of myself running back to the Giants with this bit of secret information.

Ringo played. He played well. I could see his arm hanging limply several times during the game. But he did not allow it to adversely affect his blocking. And Green Bay won its second straight championship game against the Giants, 16-7.

Afterward, I went to see Ringo. He said: "Thanks. It hurts like hell."

Ringo was to run afoul of Lombardi's peculiar philosophy of loyalty and allegiance two years later. After the 1963 season, Ringo was having difficulty negotiating a new contract with the Packers. He was doing it himself—head-to-head with Vince—because the coach had made no secret of his hatred for agents and players who used them.

One afternoon, a man visited the Packers offices and introduced himself to Lombardi as Jim Ringo's new agent. Lombardi scowled. "Wait here a minute," he said. Then he went into his office, made a telephone call, and emerged five minutes later. "You are in the wrong office," he told the agent. "I have just traded Mr. Ringo to the Philadelphia Eagles."

Ringo played four more seasons.

In 1965, 1966, and 1967, the Packers won NFL titles. They also won the first two Super Bowl championships, following the 1966 and 1967 seasons. Ringo was with the Eagles when he should have been with the Packers. His decision to hire an agent cost him at least—remember, at least—$65,000 in additional income from post-season play.

But at least his arm was all right.

Football players have been known to attempt inflicting personal damage on outspoken newspapermen. Jerry Green of the *Detroit News* was once chased around the field in the old Tiger Stadium by a particularly enraged offensive lineman. Pat Livingston of the *Pittsburgh Press* had a doubleheader—he was forcibly evicted from a locker room by head coach Bill Austin, and he was spat upon by defensive tackle Mean Joe Greene.

The problem with most such spoiled football brats can probably be found under the classification of Arrested Development. Star athletes have been coddled and sheltered since their early teens. Depending on the college they attend, the coach may well demand and receive a hands-off policy from the local newspapers. Woody Hayes at Ohio State is a classic example, for many of the athletes who left his nest and embarked on a pro football career have been found singularly incapable of dealing with criticism.

No one could write negatively about these stars, because no one knew them. In addition, few of them have ever had to deal with a losing season. Thus, when both factors coincide, they reach a flash point with incredible swiftness. To write for public consumption that "so-and-so is not having a particularly outstanding season" is often grounds for bitter recriminations and veiled or overt threats.

But the fans, clearly, are made to suffer. The newspapers are their access to the players and coaches, to the inside bits of news and observations not offered by the television people. When a player refuses to speak to a particular newsman—or, in the case of more than a few superstars, with any newsman—he is denying the fan his right to know what is happening.

It usually does no good to explain to the player or coach the financial chain that shows that their salaries are ultimately paid by the fan. Players and coaches have very little regard for fans or newspapermen, and would be thrilled and delighted with total isolation from both.

If the other side of that coin was in force—a total isolation from the players as the choice of the fans—there would be no need for networks to shell out big dollars for the right to televise games, there would be no daily newspaper coverage of the local team, and pro football players would become as popular as toilet bowl manufacturers. But don't try to explain this to the more militant athletes. They either won't understand or will refuse to believe they have not been given a divine right to live as modern-day aristocrats.

Newspapermen try to ask questions that fans would like to have answered. This is why many athletes do not enjoy appearing at public functions, for many times they are asked direct, sometimes pointed, questions.

"Why can't you cover Mel Gray of the Cardinals?"

"Why has the team not won a championship in ten years?"

"What kind of coach is Joe Blow?"

"What do you think of the draft choices this year?"

"How come John Doe plays ahead of you?"

Much nicer, indeed, to be asked: "What sort of pattern did you run on that touchdown catch?" But not so good to ask: "On that deep post pattern, when you beat the safety by fifteen yards, what happened to cause you to drop the ball?" There are times when one asks questions and receives gracious answers. Most of those times are during periods immediately following a victory.

Yet, on the other hand, fans are not always decent and understanding. Their money, they often feel, entitles them to manifest any type of behavior. There have been instances of fans physically assaulting players. Booth Lusteg was once beaten in Buffalo on a Sunday night after he missed a field goal that cost the Bills a victory.

In 1969, having written a magazine article on the Green Bay Packers, I received a fan letter via the magazine. It was sent by a paragon of culture from Bessemer, Alabama, and it was congratulatory in nature.

"Dear Mr. Klein," it read. "I really liked your storey [sic] about the Packers. What I liked most was that you didn't mentione [sic] Bart Starr very much. It is about time people knew the real Bart Starr. Do you know that he actually wanted the University [one assumes Alabama] to admit nigras [sic] when he went to school here? That is why the team didn't win a game in his last season . . . the players wouldn't play for him. And I know someone who went to visit him in

Greenbay [sic] and saw a nigra [sic] couple eating dinner at his table? Keep up the good work."

This could not go unanswered. So from my newspaper's files (sorry, boss) I took an eight-by-ten glossy photograph of Matt Snell, then a fullback with the New York Jets. Matt is a delightful man, but he will never win a beauty contest. Matt is also black. The photograph was a full-face closeup. Matt was perspiring. I clipped off the bottom margin, which identified him, and signed the glossy as an athlete would:

"Thanks for the note. Best in Sports. Dave Klein."

Then I mailed it to the mental midget in Alabama. I would have paid real money to see his face when he opened the envelope. (Snell and Starr, incidentally, were among the most cooperative and gracious pro football players of all time, at least from a newspaperman's point of view.)

The newspaperman's job is simply to report. Whether he is assigned to local politics or local industry or local sports, he is first a reporter, second an observer, then an opinion-giver. To perform as a reporter means to perform as an observer, but to be able to offer constructive, valid opinions is harder. The difference between a fan and a newspaperman is—or should be—impartiality.

In order to do a meaningful job, the correspondent must not take sides. This is a rule all too frequently violated; to many correspondents there is nothing quite as obnoxious as cheering in the press box. Newspapermen, in many cities, appear to have confused the identity of their employers. They refer to teams as "we" and to their newspaper superiors as "they."

Not to belabor the point, it should make no difference whether one is assigned to a team that wins or

loses. Reporting what happened is the only requirement. The more experienced newspaperman may also
offer an opinion about why it happened or what should
have happened. But coaches and players are paid regardless of what is written; so, too, are newspapermen.

The only allegiance a reporter should have is to his
nameless and faceless readers; they must get a fair and
unbiased account of an event. If they are given a series
of excuses, it is unsatisfactory. If they are given a one-
sided view of a game, they are being cheated.

Coaches have a difficult time with this truth. They
consider the correspondents assigned to their teams as
either friends or enemies. To cover up for a loss means
being a friend; to tell a painful truth means being an
enemy. Neutrality is never recognized; if it is, it isn't
understood or condoned.

Some years ago, when the New England Patriots
were terrible and the Washington Redskins were for-
midable, George Allen's bunch went to Foxboro,
Mass., to inflict great damage on the collective body of
the woebegone home team. But, as they say, a funny
thing happened to the Redskins on their way to
success. They snatched defeat from the jaws of victory
with a succession of improbable errors, and presented
New England with an unexpected win.

And George blamed the press. More specifically, he
blamed George Solomon of the *Washington Post*, who
was not a Woodward or a Bernstein, but nevertheless
an efficient and thorough reporter.

Coach George accused reporter George of lulling the
veteran Redskins into a state of lethargy. Coach
George indicated that since reporter George had been
writing all week just how bad the Patriots were, the
Redskins believed it, took his words to heart, and
didn't try very hard.

It was, Allen asserted, Solomon's fault. To which Solomon wisely responded: "Say, coach. If I write how tough next week's opponent is, and then you win, will you carry me off the field on your shoulders?"

But the greatest manipulator of the press—and in this category a champion is significant because the runners-up include the likes of Allen, Arnsparger, John McKay, and Al Davis—was Vince Lombardi.

First, let us make a few statements about Green Bay. There is a serious suspicion that there is no Green Bay. Many believe that it is simply a stage prop, and as soon as a season has concluded, all the storefronts are torn down and everybody goes back to the dairy farms. Let it also be said that Green Bay, 120 miles or so from Milwaukee, has one newspaper. It's a perfectly nice little newspaper, but the Packers are its only major sports subject. When they were THE PACKERS, no one dared to criticize the team or the coach. Especially not the coach, since he had reached such a level of canonization in that little town that a telephone call from him could have ended a man's career.

Lord, the things Lombardi did. What he referred to as "stupid questions" were never answered. He merely stared down at the interrogator with a hard, cold glare. When the Packers reached the first Super Bowl, there was a mass press conference two days prior to the slaughter of Kansas City. Lombardi wasn't very happy with this in the first place, but he was not prepared to put up with any nonsense, especially not from the sole representative of Green Bay's sole newspaper. So when the reporter asked a question, Lombardi stared, as if stunned by the man's temerity. "When I agreed to let you come here," he said, in a Los Angeles hotel ballroom seating roughly three hundred newsmen, "you promised you wouldn't ask any stupid questions. And that, my friend, was a stupid question." Before our eyes, the man shrank. So did Lombardi.

After a rare defeat in Milwaukee, the Packers' second home (they play some games there each season), a reporter visited The Legend in his suite in the Pfister Hotel. He'd ask a question and Lombardi would flay his hide. Over and over. Finally, Marie Lombardi came to the reporter's defense. "Vin, you just can't talk to him like that," she protested.

Lombardi erupted. "Marie, you go to your room!" he yelled. "I'll handle the press." Lombardi always handled the press.

But, being from Brooklyn and having served as an assistant coach with the Giants, he seemed to have a soft spot in his granite heart for New York newsmen. In 1965, having been forced to spend ten consecutive days in Green Bay between the Packers' Conference playoff victory over Baltimore and the next week's NFL championship game with Cleveland, the late Milton Gross of the *New York Post* decided to kill time late one afternoon. He entered the hotel's barber shop. "I'm sorry, sir," said the solitary barber, "but it's almost four o'clock and we close at four o'clock. You'll have to come back tomorrow."

Then Lombardi walked in. "Cut his hair," snapped The Legend, "and then cut mine." Needless to say, Gross got his haircut. So did The Legend. But Gross had to pay.

Another time, a local Associated Press reporter discovered that fullback Jim Taylor had played out his option. He approached Lombardi at practice one day for comment. "'Yeah, Taylor is playing out his option,' said The Legend. 'He wants to finish out his career at home, in New Orleans.' When he told me that, I asked who he thought was going to block for him. 'Oh, by the way. If you write about this, I'll bar you from the locker room and the practice field.' "

The kid wrote it. The kid was barred. It took a stern directive from the Commissioner's Office to undo the ban.

Lombardi also put out a timetable that indicated when the press would be allowed to telephone him at home during the week. It was between the hour of five and six P.M. No earlier, no later.

A Milwaukee reporter tried the mansion at 5:55 one day. The phone was busy. At 6:01, he tried again. Vince answered. The reporter said hello. Vince said: "It's after six. Good-bye." Click.

9. In the NFL, a Draft

"Let me tell you how the NFL teams do their drafting. First they pick the All-Americans. Then they go cutesy and take basketball players. Finally, when nobody else is left, they start picking the real football players."
> —Stan White, Baltimore linebacker (17th round)

"If the Giants really wanted Rocky Thompson, they could have still taken him in the third round. I can't believe they took him first."
> —Gil Brandt, Vice President, Dallas Cowboys

"Every time a first-round draft choice washes out, I get angry. Every time a free agent kid proves he's a player, I get angry. Every time we flop on a first-round choice and sign a free agent who makes it big, I should fire somebody."
> —Andy Robustelli, Director of Operations, Giants

Welcome to the draft, which occupies the largest room by far in the House of Fantasy that pro football has built.

The draft is an annual and arbitrary dispersal of all the football-playing college seniors in the country. It is the lifeline of the National Football League. It is the process by which teams acquire new talent, young talent, future stars.

It is carefully planned and plotted. Literally millions of dollars are spent each year on research. Scouts spend the better part of a year on the road visiting colleges, picking the brains of coaches, examining players, and timing, weighing, measuring, and testing them psychologically. There is no truth to the rumor that they also check teeth and breeding capabilities. Then dawns the big day. The draft is held.

Teams select in an inverse order of their previous season's record, i.e., the team with the worst record picks first, the team with the next worst record picks second, and so on and so forth. In recent years, so-called selection ties have been broken by calculating the records of the opponents, and the 2-12 team that played a weaker schedule wins the earlier pick.

The teams are well-prepared. They know everything about every eligible college player. They know more about the kid than do his mother and father, maybe even more than his girlfriend. They know exactly what he will do, how well he will be able to do it, how soon before he will assume the mantle of starting player, how well he will interact with the veterans.

The hell they do.

The draft is the biggest crap game this side of the New York Stock Exchange. You rolls the dice and you takes your chances . . . you pays your money and you takes your chances . . . you follows your scouts and you takes your chances. . . .

"When we go twelve rounds." said Al Davis of the Oakland Raiders, one of the more fortunate rollers in the league, "we're hoping to find three or four players and not too many embarrassments. That means we're hoping to get lucky. You have to get lucky to draft well. All your information and research simply allows you to make selections the other teams won't laugh at. They've all got the same information, the same data. If the kid stinks, they're all relieved. But they can't laugh at you. If you didn't take the kid, they would have."

Anyway, there have been some magnificent first-round mistakes. For example:

●Defensive tackle Harold Lucas, of Michigan State. He was drafted number 1 by the St. Louis Cardinals. He was six three and he weighed 330 pounds. He signed a contract that called for a bonus-upon-signing of $350,000 (almost a thousand dollars a pound). Three days after summer training camp started, Harold's feelings were hurt by an assistant coach, who said he was too fat. Harold left camp—with a ton of money. He never returned.

●Quarterback Terry Baker, of Oregon State. He was the 1962 Heisman Trophy winner. He was Frank Merriwell reincarnate. He was everything the All-American should be. He had the scouts drooling. Happily, the Rams had the worst record in the NFL in 1962. It was 1-12-1. They had the first choice, and almost without hesitation they drafted Terry Baker. Better they should have had more hesitation. Baker was disappointing. He spent three seasons with Los Angeles and the best thing he ever did was pick up his check.

●Bob Ferguson, Ohio State fullback, and Dick Leftridge, West Virginia fullback. Both were drafted by the Pittsburgh Steelers—Ferguson in 1962, Leftridge in 1966. Both had performed with a delightful violence as collegians, and both became All-America selections. Both weighed 225 pounds, or more. Both were fantastic disappointments. But the Steelers deserve a measure of credit. They stuck with it, and the next time they

drafted a fullback in the first round (1972), it was
Franco Harris.

•Special mention must be made of the New York
Giants, who have drafted with as much total foolishness and bad luck as any team in the league. This is
not to downgrade many of the Giants' earlier top
selections, which included Frank Gifford and Kyle
Rote and . . . well, Frank Gifford and Kyle Rote. On
the other hand, they have claimed as their top
selections athletes such as Joe Don Looney, Dick
Skelly, Don Davis, Francis Peay, Rocky Thompson,
Wayne Walton, Eldridge Small, Larry Jacobson, Bob
Gaiters, and Glynn Griffing. The reason you haven't
heard of them or don't remember their names is that
they were all mistakes. It can be calculated that the
monies paid out to these nonperformers approached
one million. Clearly, there is much to be said for a
perennially sold-out stadium.

But all teams have made grievous errors, and all
teams have experienced much good fortune, and most
teams have actually been right on occasion.

The draft, which began in 1936, used to be
conducted on a rather informal basis. Team owners
would meet in a predetermined town (New York,
Chicago, and Philadelphia shared most of the
meetings), laden with college football magazines.

They would then draft for as long as there were
names left unclaimed (which is how, in 1953, the
Giants managed to claim offensive tackle Rosey
Brown, whose name is in the Hall of Fame, in the
twenty-seventh round. That's twenty-seventh). There
was very little scouting or in-person viewing because
there was little cash available for so frivolous a hobby.

Thus the newspapers, radio, and magazines were
largely responsible for the drafting of college players.

The smaller colleges, which were unrecognized by the media and therefore the owners, were left to offer their young men as free agents. Included in this group is Hall of Fame safety Emlen Tunnell, who showed up at the Giants' offices in midtown Manhattan one day and asked for a tryout. The Giants agreed to look at him, which is how they came to earn the reputation of being a canny, clever, and far-thinking organization that scoured the countryside for talent.

There was, as well, less difficulty in drafting then. Most of the blacks were eliminated. The NFL had almost as rigid a color barrier as did major league baseball, but since professional football was looked upon as a profession just a notch higher than pimping, no one really cared.

George Preston Marshall, who owned the Washington Redskins, was one of the strong, all-white supporters. This was, he felt, in the cause of practicality, since his all-white fans were drawn from Maryland, the District of Columbia, and Virginia.

His stance on race also became a source of gallows-like humor among the press in Washington, as those gentlemen waited for old George to make a mistake and draft a black. But George was a dogged and determined sort. He never slipped.

One of his closest friends in Washington was a sportswriter—a friendship that came to an abrupt end when George learned that he and his friend had been seeing the same woman for more than five years. But before this rift-due-to-passion occurred, the sportswriter managed to draft a black for the Redskins.

"George kept promising me that I'd be able to make a draft selection for the Redskins," remembers the sportswriter. "Each year I'd nag and pester him and finally he agreed. And did I do my homework! Lord, I stayed up for a week, researching all the smaller schools, since I was sure George wouldn't know a damned thing about them. I wanted to find a legitimate football player, of course. I wanted to get a black on the team.

"Well, the draft finally came around and when it got into the lower rounds George turned to me and said: 'This is it, my friend, this is your round.' I played it cool. I waited until it was our turn, listing the names of the players taken just ahead of us, hoping my man wouldn't be drafted. Well, he wasn't. And when they said 'Washington' I was ready. I shouted out his name and it was recorded and that did it.

"Then George asked me what I knew about the kid. 'Well, George,' I said, 'he's six three and he weighs 215, and he's a fullback and he runs the hundred in ten flat and he had a great career at old Oshkosh State and scored fifty touchdowns.'

"George beamed. 'Oh, and George . . .' I added. George looked up, still smiling. 'George, he's as black as the ace of spades.'

"I thought old George was going to choke himself. But he managed to keep the team all-white. He traded the kid—for nothing—before he even tried to sign him. I'd like to say the kid became a star, but he didn't. But he was the first black the Washington Redskins ever drafted."

Washington, first in war and first in peace, was also last in integrating its football team. The Redskins didn't field a black until 1962, when they drafted the late Ernie Davis of Syracuse (and then traded his rights to Cleveland for Bobby Mitchell and rookie Leroy Jackson, both blacks).

Today, of course, the computer has taken over, and nowhere in professional football has it made more of an impact than in the scouting and drafting of players. But there are two basic flaws in computer drafting. One involves the difficulty of ascertaining grades for all the intangibles such as courage, loyalty, pain threshold, and determination that make up a football player. The scouts lump all of these, and more, under a heading called "Heart." But, at best, judging the "heart" of a college senior is speculative.

The other difficulty is known by its initials in the computer industry—GIGO. This acronym stands for "Garbage In, Garbage Out" and it refers to those who feed the computer its daily ration of data.

Not many football people are qualified computer technicians, but not many computer technicians are qualified football people. So we are confronted with a kind of credibility gap. What we are presented with is erroneous and/or incomplete programming of the hardware, which, in all too many instances, forces the machinery to reject those who are football players but an inch or two shy of "standard" or a second or two slower than "standard." The football folks have buried themselves in a quagmire of print-outs. They have also buried several players.

We should digress for a moment to explore the colorful language used by many of the old-time scouts, most of whom still scour the countryside for talent, but whose knowledge is homogenized by the machines into which their reports are fed.

•"He couldn't pour piss out of a boot if the directions were printed on the heel." This indicates, rather obviously, a decided lack of intelligence on the part of the scouted player.

•"He pisses ice water." This player is cool under pressure.

•"He's a rural runner." The player wastes too much time scampering around in the backfield.

•"Looks like Tarzan but plays like Jane." Clearly, this player is somewhat short on courage.

•"He stands on two bricks to kick a duck in the ass." We are now discussing a player said to be too short.

•"He's six five with the heart of a dwarf." Again, this player lacks intestinal fortitude.

•"He sweats well." Here is a hard-worker. A hustler.

•"He can catch a BB at midnight." This receiver has praiseworthy hands.

•"What he does best is kill the grass." A nonactive player who stands around too much.

•"I asked him if he had any hobbies. He said he played the piano. I asked him how long. He said six feet." Another description of a none-too-bright athlete.

•"He was born on March ninth and tenth." This is an extremely large player.

•"When he goes out to dinner, he gets a bowl of milk." This player, a "pussycat," has a courage problem.

And so forth.

Another error made in the scouting of players, and made by even the most intensive of teams, is the lack of two or three reviews of an athlete. "We timed a kid in spring practice," says Jimmy Garrett, who has been a part of pro football as a scout, assistant coach, and head coach for more than a decade, "and he ran a lousy 5.1 in the forty. It wasn't satisfactory, so he got a very low rating. When it got close to the draft, we felt that every team had also discounted him, but we knew he still had a good season and his coach felt he could play. So we sent someone to time him again. He ran the forty in 4.8, which is an excellent time considering the kid was a linebacker. We drafted him. Then we asked him if he knew why he ran so poorly the first time. He said, 'Yeah, coach, I had a hamstring pull.' " The player was D. D. Lewis, who has been a starter for Dallas for five seasons.

One of the most successful scouts isn't a scout at all, nor does he work for any NFL team. His scouting began as a hobby and now he sells his reports to pro teams as well as to interested fans.

Joel Buchsbaum is a twenty-two-year-old from Brooklyn. His publication service is called "Around the Draft Table," and he offers up to a dozen publications each year, capped by a seventy-five page "Scouts Notebook" that sells for fifteen dollars.

"The scouts who work for teams just don't do things right," he contends. "It's wrong, it doesn't make sense, and it's plain stupid. Each year every NFL club spends a fortune on scouting. When a scout goes to a school, he doesn't just watch one game and file his report, he spends hours studying films of at least four games to make sure he has a good line on the player's ability. He also talks to the coaches and trainers about the boy. When he's done he can tell you how many cavities a kid has in his mouth . . . that is, if he has any teeth left. All that is great and thorough and I applaud teams for their effort.

"However, what I stand firmly opposed to is this: Most schools hold one Scouts Day in the spring. Each pro prospect runs two or three forties and that's the time he has to live with. Two years ago I talked to a friend about California linebacker Rob Swenson. I said I saw some film and the kid looked like a better prospect than Richard Wood. My friend told me to forget Swenson, he's just too slow. He only ran a 5.2

on Scouts Day. So what happened? Swenson turned up in a Denver uniform in 1975. The Broncos invited him to a free agent camp and he ran 4.8.

"This year [1977] we have many illogical cases. Let's take Miami [Florida] defensive back Willie Jenkins. He's five eleven and 190 and ran a 4.75 on Scouts Day. Plays super, but he's just too slow to play the corner as a pro or to be drafted too high. But wait a minute. The kid ran a verified 9.6 in high school. How the hell does he stay with the 4.5 guys if he's a 4.75? Why did scouts estimate him at 4.5 for their top-fifty junior lists the year before and rank him the third best defensive back in the South?

"Simple. They made a mistake when they timed him in that 4.75 forty. In a business where your job is to cut the amount of mistakes to the bare minimum, one timing day leaves a huge margin for error. Much too huge . . . and much too unfair to the players involved."

By the time a player is actually drafted, the one individual responsible for the choice is difficult to pinpoint.

"When I took over with the Giants," said Andy Robustelli, who was hired to pull the team out of its ten-year-long famine, "I tried to find out who was responsible for some of the really disgraceful draft picks. You know what? Nobody knew. It's nonsense. The kid just didn't get drafted anonymously. One man had to have the final say. But there were no records.

"Now, that's one of the things I have changed. When we draft a kid now I'll know exactly whose recommendation did it. If we get too many bad picks, I can go to the guy and say something. Or get some explanation. Or fire him." Clearly, then, the team with the successful drafting record is the one with the most astute scouts. Or the luckiest scouts.

Much of the reason behind draft success is the ability of the head coach and the personnel director to communicate. "I know what we want, because Don Shula tells me," says Bob Beathard, Miami's former Director of Player Personnel. "For a while, we were drafted way down in each round, because we had so many winning seasons. But there are more than a handful of outstanding players. You know, sometimes I think we get too restrictive, or too damn demanding. If there's only one O. J. Simpson some year, that doesn't mean there aren't any other good running backs.

"Sometimes another theory works, especially for a team that already has fairly decent talent. There is a certain kind of player whom we call a future. He has all the necessary skills, size, and drive, but maybe he's from a small school and didn't get all the specialized coaching he needed . . . or maybe he didn't start playing football until he got to college . . . or maybe he was hurt for a couple of years and never learned the things he had to learn. We try to project that kid, based on an average rate of progress, and if we think he can become an outstanding player, we'll take a chance on him and draft him high. Maybe even on the first round. That's one way to get around picking low every year."

Miami has made three such first-round selections in recent years. Their names are Donald Reese (defensive end), Darryl Carlton (offensive tackle), and Kim Bokamper (linebacker). Reese and Carlton were starters in 1976, and Bokamper, a '76 rookie who had been a defensive end in college, so impressed the usually taciturn Shula that he was moved to say: "This kid is the greatest athlete I've ever coached." Bokamper suffered a knee injury and missed the entire season, but Shula admitted that "he would definitely have been a starter, and I'm sure he will be one, as well as an all-pro, for a long, long time." He was both—starter and star—in 1977.

The search for players has, in the past decade, taken on all the earmarks of a Runyonesque adventure. "Everybody knows where all the obvious players are," said Jack Butler, one-time all-pro safety and later a Pittsburgh Steelers' scout. "The easiest job in this business is to pick number ones. You almost can't miss, because you have a ton of data and a pile of in-person scouting reports and the opinions of scores of people and cans full of game films.

"Given all that information, my grandmother could score pretty well on the first round, and probably on the second. Then it gets tougher. You have to figure out why a kid who stands six five and weighs maybe 260 didn't play well. More important, you have to decide if he can play well. So many intangibles enter into it that you're guessing. Honest to God, you're guessing.

"But you can miss a lot of good players in the draft. Every team in the league has missed them, every year. Sometimes a kid needs a kick in the ass and sometimes he needs a pat on the back and sometimes he just needs a chance to play. And sometimes he has to be moved to another position.

"Let's take a player. Let's say he's the kind who needs to feel loved and wanted. He needs praise from the coach. He looks up to the coach and almost identifies him as a father figure. So let's assume the kid had a rotten senior year . . . or a rotten college career . . . because when he needed a kiss on the forehead he got a kick in the butt. He sulked. He brooded. He never had the attention he needed that would have extracted all the talent and desire he had all along.

"So you figure out which kid can play and which kid

is simply a dog who took advantage of his size to get a free ride in college? You can go nuts. But if you guess right, you've got a star. At least a starter. And that's what your job is, to find players who can play. If a kid needs a nursemaid, give it to him. They're all different. But first you have to find them."

Dallas and Kansas City have sent expeditions to foreign countries in search of soccer players able to make the transition to placekickers. Players such as Toni Fritsch, Pete, and brother Charlie, Gogolak, Chester Marcol, Jan Stenerud, Efren Herrara, John Walker, Garo Yepremian, and the Mike-Meyer brothers, Nick and Steve, acquired their placekicking talents playing soccer, either in other lands or as a result of their ethnic origin and inclination.

"When Yepremian first showed up in camp," said Alex Karras, who was with the Detroit Lions when the Cypriot was discovered, "the little bastard didn't even know the game. All he could do was kick the ball and he didn't even know why he was doing that. But then he learned a little bit about football, and when he made a field goal he'd come running off the field, yelling: 'I keek a touchdown . . . I keek a touchdown.' "

Garo ultimately found his way to Miami, and for years provided the Dolphins with accurate placekicking.

The New England Patriots embarked on a voyage wistfully called "The Search For Superfoot" and came up with Walker, an English soccer player. "First we taught him the game," said Peter Hadhazy, then the team's assistant general manager. "But we didn't need to get technical with him. What difference did it make if he knew what the strongside safety had to do? We taught him that a field goal is three points and a conversion is one point and that the rules said he wasn't allowed to miss anything we let him kick. He bought that. John kicked well for us."

But those are not drafted players. Those are finds, true gems that appear out of the blue and fill a position. The lower rounds of the draft hold far more intrigue, because every player chosen still has the chance of becoming a starter, just as the top selections do. Yet they are all up for grabs. To the fortunate go the laurels.

The 1964 college draft was perhaps the most productive of all the Great NFL Body Snatches. The first round produced names such as Dick Butkus, Gale Sayers, Joe Namath, Craig Morton, Ken Willard, Tucker Frederickson, Mike Curtis, and Donny Anderson.

The second round produced Roy Jefferson, Lance Rentzel, Ralph Neely, and Walter Johnson.

The third round? Fred Biletnikoff, Kent McCloughan, Chuck Mercein, Jim Norton, and Bobby Maples.

And later on . . . much later on . . . an inordinate number of future heroes were to be found. The sixth round turned up Gary Garrison and Al Atkinson. In the seventh came Dick Gordon, Brig Owens, Junior Coffey, Tony Guillory, and Bob Kowalkowski. And in the eighth round came Willie Williams and Mike Howell. Tom Neville and Jerry Smith were products of the ninth round. Rick Redman came out of the tenth; Ernie Koy, Frank Molden, Jethro Pugh, Jim Kearney, from the eleventh; Ernie Kellerman and Mike Tilleman from the twelfth; Spider Lockhart and Dave Osborn from the thirteenth; Olen Underwood and Cannonball Butler from the fourteenth; Otis Taylor, Roy Hilton, Larry Gagner, and Chuck Hurston from the fifteenth.

And there were still diamonds in the rough like

quarterback Steve Tensi and wide receiver Frank Pitts found in the sixteenth round. Chris Hanburger, of all people, was drafted by Washington in the eighteenth round, along with Bob Howard, Marty Amsler, Mike Ciccolella, Karl Sweetan, and Dick Arrington. Roy Shivers and Barry Brown were products of the nineteenth round and players such as Ralph Kurek, Craig Fertig, Cosmo Iacavazzi, and George Wilson brought up the rear of what was then a twenty-round draft. By actual count, more than one hundred of the players drafted by the NFL teams that year played at least one season as professionals.

And, of course, we haven't mentioned names such as Henry Carr, Jim Nance, Tom Myers, Fred Hill, Marty Schottenheimer, Bob Svihus, Johnny Roland, John Henderson, Ed Flanagan, Jimmy Sidle, and Doug Woodleif, who were drafted in the fourth and fifth rounds.

What does it prove? In a good year, with the crop tall and plentiful, every team can come up with players. In an off-year, only the smart ones can produce in quantity.

"I remember once," Jimmy Garrett said, "I was working as a scout for Dallas, and I was on a timing trip. You know, I'd get to a school and line up the players we were interested in and time them in the forty. It was a lot of work, there were a lot of players, and my airline schedule was very tight. Finally, I just ran out of time. I flew into a city and I had an hour to get out and I couldn't get to the campus and back in time. There was only one player. So I called the school and they drove him to the airport and we cleared a corridor and, in shoes, the kid ran a few forties for me. We got a lot of strange looks, and we never even drafted the kid."

There was the time the Giants sent a scout out on a timing mission. When he was finished, he raced for a telephone and called New York. "I found the greatest draft prospects in the world," he yelled. "Just listen to these times." He proceeded to rattle off clockings of 3.8, 3.9, 4. flat, and 4.1 for the forty-yard dash.

The voice in New York had one suggestion. "Go back and walk off the stretch of track." He did. It was thirty yards long. Not forty.

Indeed, the forty-yard dash used as the infallible measure of scouting seems a trifle overrated. There are few times in any game when even the running backs or the wide receivers will have to run that far during a single play. Linemen will almost never find themselves sprinting forty yards. In actuality, the forty is the result of a computation of how far a player on the special teams—especially the punting and kickoff team—will have to run in order to get to the punt-receiver when the ball does. Most NFL punters average very close to forty yards per kick, perhaps ranging from forty-three to thirty-eight. There is no other reason for the forty-yard dash to be held in such high esteem by the scouts, nor does it make much sense to disqualify a college player whose time isn't up to standards.

"They should be more interested in a time for fifteen or twenty yards," said former Rams' defensive tackle Merlin Olsen, who retired in 1977 after fifteen all-pro seasons. "I never ran forty yards in all the games I played. My time would have been absolutely disgraceful. But I didn't have to run forty yards."

Charley Harper, a journeyman offensive lineman who played seven seasons with the New York Giants, never had any speed. He considered that one of his assets. "When I was first scouted," he said, "and they had me run the forty, I ran my ass off and I got timed in 5.5. It was awful. When I played in the NFL, I'm sure I had gotten even slower. And you know what? I was so slow I couldn't commit myself to the first move a defensive lineman made. And since the first move is usually a decoy, I was right where he wanted to go anyway. What the hell does a lineman need sprinter's speed for to block a guy six inches away from him?"

The purists will yelp. They will say a pulling guard must have such-and-such speed. But most pulling guards do have adequate or even spectacular speed—for just as long as their duties require. "No guard in the world," says Minnesota's Ed White, "runs a forty-yard pull. Even if I'm crossing over [right guard pulling out for a sweep to the left] it's maybe ten, maybe fifteen yards. And I know I can go like hell because it's not an endurance race. I won't have to run forty. If we're lucky, the ball carrier will do that. But how many gains are there over forty yards in a game, or in a season? A handful. The forty is just somebody's idea of what a player should run. It doesn't make any sense, and it doesn't have any validity."

White is an all-pro. He weighs 280. If he could run a 4.8 forty, he'd be the damndest wide receiver or defensive back anybody ever saw.

All right. Certain players pass all the tests, run in the prescribed clockings, and have the proper height and weight. They will become draft choices. Some of them will even become football players. What of the rest? What of the ones who are not drafted, who are rejected as too slow or short, too light or raw, or even, in the sublime arrogance of scouts who can't spell, too stupid? They become free agents. And they are far better off.

"If you are not drafted by, say, the fifth round, then

the best thing you can be is a free agent," says Frank Ross, who has worked as Hank Stram's assistant-in-charge-of-everything in both Kansas City and New Orleans. "The money goes to the kids in the first five rounds . . . and to the free agents. The poor bastards in between have no choice and no negotiating power. It's a general rule, I think, that free agents will get more money, at least more front money, than the lower draftees."

There is a why to all this. The kid drafted, say, in the ninth round has no choice. Teams must figure that a ninth-round pick isn't going to have much of a chance to make the team. It's a delightful Catch-22 affair—if he were capable of making it, he would have been drafted higher. But he might be capable of making it, which is why he wasn't ignored and allowed to become a free agent, because he might make it for some other team and become a source of embarrassment.

But this Catch-22 goes even further. Those who were passed up, and become free agents, may be hotly pursued by several teams in the league. It's another chance, you see. It's an additional opportunity to make up for the mistakes that most teams will admit—privately—they always make in the draft.

This scurrying became even more widespread—and more potentially fruitful—in 1977, when the NFL draft was shortened by five rounds to a total of twelve, as part of the overall collective bargaining agreement worked out after a three-year period of negotiating between the NFL Players Association and the NFL Management Council (representing the owners).

A free agent will begin to receive telephone calls the day after the draft is completed.

"Mike, would you be willing to sign with us?"

"Well, coach, you'll have to call my agent. We've already gotten offers from the Bears, Giants, Raiders, and Vikings."

"Oh? Well, tell me how much you need?"

The free agent is in a far better position than the lower draft choices. Say he's a linebacker, and say he's contacted by a team loaded with young, successful line-backers. He is free to tell that team to disappear. But if that team drafted a linebacker on the eleventh round, the kid can't say anything but "thank you, sir," while his private reveries might include the words "why me, Lord?"

The free agent is able to pick and choose. He will probably pick and choose a team with lousy linebackers, for that will increase his chances of becoming a professional and cash in on a fat contract and lucrative fringe benefits. And he will get money . . . more money than most of the drafted players on that same team.

Why? Because he can go elsewhere, and the eleventh-round selection cannot. Because he can say, "You called me and I have other alternatives," and the eleventh-round selection cannot. Because he can say, "Oakland is going to give me ten thousand for sign-ing," and the eleventh-round selection cannot.

And because of the aforementioned variances in the scouting and drafting process, the free agent does have a real chance of making a team.

In the 1976 season there were former free agents in the NFL such as Drew Pearson and Cliff Harris of Dallas, both of whom were voted to that season's all-pro squad; John Smith and Mike Patrick, the placekicker and punter for the New England Patriots; Coy Bacon, the Pro Bowl defensive end of the Cincinnati Bengals; Toni Linhart and Nelson Munsey, starters for the playoff Baltimore Colts; and Conrad

Dobler—"Dirty Dobler"—of the St. Louis Cardinals, an all-pro guard.

This says absolutely nothing, of course, about the most famous free agent of them all, quarterback John Unitas of the Baltimore Colts, a kid from the Pittsburgh sandlots cut by the then-doormat hometown Steelers, who had also signed him as a free agent.

Finally, the head coaches of the league will spice up every draft by issuing the same statements over and over, as if trying to prove their profound wisdom and talents as discoverers of unrefined talent. There is a playbook full of tiresome clichés that are dusted off each year at draft time. To wit:

"We were amazed to find him still available on the twelfth round." Translation: The coach was amazed to see that one of his scouts picked the stiff.

"He needs to work on his upper body strength." Translation: He's a pussycat and if I can find out who gave him a good scouting report I'll break his legs.

"For a running back, he has exceptional hands." Translation: He can't run worth a damn, but maybe I can make a receiver out of him so I won't have to be embarrassed by cutting him in camp.

"He was rated fourth on our list of tight ends." Translation: The other three were broads, and stronger.

"We went for the best available athlete." Translation: All the football players were gone, but this kid plays boccie.

"He could be a sleeper." Translation: If he ever wakes up long enough to play a game, I'll have a reason to cut him.

"He may be raw, but he can really throw the ball." Translation: The kid's no more a quarterback than I am, but what the hell was left?

"He has more speed than any of our running backs." Translation: Which probably makes up for the fact that he's a terminal coward.

"He had a great sophomore season, and based on that we had to take a chance." Translation: His college coach said the kid was great until somebody popped him, and then he quit.

"If he didn't get that baseball offer, he would have been drafted much higher." Translation: The offer from baseball was that he should try football.

And so forth.

Finally, one thought comes to the surface: The NFL claims that the draft is designed to enable the weaker teams to become stronger, since by having the front-runners draft lower, an overall league balance is achieved. But if this is so, why do they allow teams to trade away draft choices? Invariably, the strong teams have a surplus of talent (surplus in this case means players who can't beat out the stars, not players guaranteed to be stars elsewhere), and so they are able to dangle these warm bodies in front of the teams who have nothing.

Then the strong teams suck up the higher draft choices owned by the weaker teams and continue to get stronger while the weaker teams find they have been seduced. In May, 1977, the hottest running back in the nation—despite what Tampa Bay believed—was Heisman Trophy winner Tony Dorsett of the University of Pittsburgh. He went to Dallas, after the Cowboys completed a trade with Seattle, which had the second choice in the first round, in exchange for Dallas' first-round choice came from San Diego, and two of the round pick and three second-round picks. The first-three second-round choices were acquired by Dallas in previous trades.

This is an example of how strong teams stay that way, and the best reason possible for preventing the trade of draft choices. The consistently weak teams must be immunized against their own stupidity.

10. Ready...Set...Think!

A man who has made millions selling insurance just isn't going to tolerate people telling him he isn't qualified to make decisions. Even if, when he buys a pro football team, he doesn't know what cleats are.

"When I was traded to the Giants, they said they were instituting a rebuilding program. Five years later, they said they were about to institute a rebuilding program. That's when I asked to be traded. They didn't have much to rebuild with anyway. Either time."
—Fran Tarkenton, 1972

"Why is it that year after year the same teams finish at the bottom, get the top draft picks, and continue to finish at the bottom? The strong teams, with low draft picks, continue to find more and more all-pros."
—Question that weak teams refuse to answer.

"Because we know what we're doing and they don't."
—Answer to above, supplied by the strong teams.

"When you ask an assistant coach to be your head coach and he turns you down to stay where he is, you had better take a look at what you offered him."

This is the bottom line: If the Bell System ran its business the way most pro football franchise owners run theirs, we would still be communicating with each other via drums and pigeons.

Mistakes are inevitable. We all make them. Ford tried to sell us the Edsel. Nixon tried to sell us a lot of things. But errors of stupidity or incompetence are less easy to forgive, and what has been a constant source of amazement to observers of the pro football scene is how owners can commit the most ridiculous gaffes and not even slow the torrent of money that pours out of their golden cornucopias.

Examples abound. The Giants left Yankee Stadium and found themselves orphans of the storm for three years, having to resort to use of the Yale Bowl in New Haven, Conn., as the site of their "home" games.

Misguided team managements insist on making trades, and thus deal away players for nothing, devastating already shaky rosters. Or owners hire unqualified scouts, who then present the beleaguered head coach with women and children. When the draft choices fail to produce, the coach is fired.

Basically, the duties of an owner are threefold:

He must hire administrators who have the proper talents and experience.

He must hire head coaches who can coach.

He must then leave these people alone, allowing them to handle the functions for which they were hired in the first place.

Winning teams fiulfill these requirements. The rest try to be accurate in the selection of personnel, but even if they do stumble into the correct decisions, they negate everything by ignoring the third dictum.

The greatest single ailment to afflict head coaches and general managers in this Disneyland of a business is owner interference. Meddling. The exercising of unwarranted authority. If an assembly-line sweathog tried to tell William Clay Ford how to manage the automobile business, he would swiftly become an unemployed assembly-line sweathog. But when William Clay Ford tells the head coach how to manage his Detroit Lions, the coach is expected to obey. If he doesn't, he swiftly becomes an unemployed head coach.

Owners are victimized by their own gigantic ego. Their egos were almost certainly vital to business success, of course, and once a man has fed his with success, it becomes difficult for others to tell him what he should do, and even more difficult for him to tolerate such advice.

"I have made fifty million dollars selling plastic pipe, young man. How dare you tell me I'm making a mistake. I know people, and I insist."

"But we can't use that quarterback, sir. He's just no damned good and we'll never win with him."

"You just use him or resign. Remember, my wife and I drafted him. Keep that in mind."

Perhaps the most famous interfering owner was Harry Wismer, who earned a public image as a nationwide radio announcer and almost as wide a private image as a bore. He was instrumental in the creation of the American Football League in 1959, and as a reward for his efforts he claimed the New York franchise, which he named the Titans.

He allowed his wife to pick some of the starters. He changed coaches at the drop of a refused request. He telephoned newsmen in the wee hours of the morning to embark on tirades against the Giants, who then were consistent winners and whose winning Wismer interpreted as an NFL "conspiracy" against his Titans and the AFL.

"I put up the money [which wasn't true, since the Titans' major problem was a humiliating lack of funds] and I pay the bills [which was also a distortion, since several Titan creditors never saw any money], so it's my privilege to decide what goes on with this team. I'll play whom I want to play and I'll hire and fire as I decide. I'm fighting an impossible battle, since the newspapers in this town are all sucking on the NFL's tit."

The zenith of zaniness occurred when Wismer and his wife rode the Titans' bench, making substitutions and calling plays. The Titans inevitably went bankrupt. So did Harry. It came as a surprise to absolutely no one.

Wismer's departure in 1963 provided entry for David "Sonny" Werblin and four equally wealthy friends, who promptly secured a new stadium (Shea), provided abundant capital, and legitimate players. The team was renamed the Jets.

The investment of the Werblin group was one million, surely one of the miraculous modern-day sports bargains. Some years later, when Werblin was bought out by his partners, his share of the stock had burgeoned to a value of nearly four million.

Werblin's first important act as head of the Titan/Jets was to hire a competent head coach, Weeb Ewbank. That was the start of a whirlwind escalation that resulted in the fabled upset victory over Baltimore in Super Bowl III on January 12, 1969.

Werblin was too smart to make the decision for a head coach on his own. Where Wismer had insisted he knew it all, Werblin admitted he knew almost nothing about the game and sought advice from experts. Ewbank was the consensus choice, compiled from the suggestions of many. It was the right one.

Too often, the first decision made by an owner—that of selecting head coach—dooms the franchise to years of chaos, failure, and lack of progress.

The favorite truism among the monied owner-clowns is that if a head coach is highly successful, his assistant coaches will be equally successful when given the chance to lead. As in many other areas, success is not often passed down from head man to assistant. Example: During the glory ride of the Green Bay Packers from 1959 through most of the 1960s, Vince Lombardi was the head coach. And every time a vacancy arose elsewhere in the league, the owner of that franchise sent for one of Lombardi's aides.

That led to the elevation to head coach of men such as Tom Fears (New Orleans), Norb Hecker (Atlanta), Bill Austin (Pittsburgh), and Phil Bengtson (Lombardi's own replacement). All were dismissed in three years or less with embarrassing won-lost records.

And this upheld the countrified commonsense theory once expounded by Clemson head coach Frank Howard, who watched one day as a bright young coach at Maryland named Tom Nugent beat the highly favored Tigers with a gimmicky kickoff-return double-handoff. Howard came to the Maryland locker room afterward to offer congratulations to Nugent and his Terrapins. "You won the game," he drawled, "and that's great. But next time I don't think you'll be close. After all, it's mighty tough to make chicken salad out of chickenshit two times in a row."

The fact was that Lombardi had assembled enough outstanding players to win almost no matter who did the coaching. In truth, those Packers might have won with any assistant coach. For Lombardi was the dominant figure.

The other owners went for glory, insisted that success will always breed success, utilized the concepts that had worked in the insurance and oil businesses, and as a result, screwed up their teams for years.

Another example of this fatal non-think can be found in Miami, where head coach Don Shula became the new Lombardi and built some of the greatest teams ever assembled, including the 1972 edition that compiled a perfect 17-0 record. His assistants soon became the objects of high-powered selling campaigns mounted by money-throwing owners. Hired away to become head coaches were Howard Schnellenberger, Bill Arnsparger, and Monte Clark.

Fired soon after their hirings were Howard Schnellenberger, Bill Arnsparger, and Monte Clark. Even Pat Peppler, who acted as unofficial general manager (because the title belonged to Shula), was hired to oversee the fortunes of the Atlanta Falcons. He, too, was fired.

Again, Shula had proved to be the dominant force, not his assistants. And, like Lombardi, he confirmed this by hiring replacement aides and continued to win. At this writing, Schnellenberger and Arnsparger had been hired back by Shula to resume their former duties as assistants.

On the other hand, there have been men who turned out a number of quality head coaches. Paul Brown is responsible for on-the-job training of men such as Ewbank, Shula, Blanton Collier, Walt Michaels, Chuck Noll, and Otto Graham, among others. Jim Lee Howell, while head coach of the Giants in the 1950s, trained such future heroes as Tom Landry, Lombardi, Allie Sherman, and Dick Nolan.

Was there a significant difference in the knowledge imparted by Brown and Howell, as compared to that offered by Lombardi and Shula? Not likely. The difference was undoubtedly in the talent level of the teams that hired and promoted the assistants and in the well-rounded backgrounds of the assistants hired, which brings up another element of coaching.

Perhaps 95 percent of all assistant coaches are waiting to become head coaches. When jobs open, these anxious assistants flood the coachless teams with résumés and applications. Many have sought the counsel of their boss, as to his opinion of the situation.

But while working as an assistant, most men acquire a deep and profound knowledge of only one part of the game. The man is a defensive line coach or an offensive backfield coach or a linebacker coach and so forth. He is not a head coach.

"When I worked for the Vikings," said Jack Patera, who became the first head coach of the expansionist Seattle Seahawks, "I was the defensive line coach. That meant I coached Alan Page, Carl Eller, Jim Marshall, and Doug Sutherland. And what did that mean? It meant all I had to do was make sure they got on the bus on Sunday mornings. I never pretended that I was responsible for the success of that front four. I simply inherited great players. But football is like anything else. It requires study, time, and experience. I'm still learning to be a head coach. So are all the other head coaches in this business."

The underlying truth here is that a man hired from the staff of another team may not have expertise in other than his specific area, and regardless of his direct experience, he had better make damned sure he hires assistants with knowledge in the other areas of the game. For the quality of the staff is the only criterion that can predict the success or failure of a head coach, assuming the team has superior players.

"When I coached the Giants," Howell said, "I had maybe the finest staff ever assembled. I would have to have been as crazy as hell to tell them what to do. I wanted them to tell me what they were going to do. How could I tell Landry about defense, or Lombardi about offense, or Sherman about theory? I couldn't. What I did was exercise authority and tie it all together. People joked that my duties involved blowing up the footballs and making curfew bed-checks. Fine. We won, didn't we?"

One of Howell's players was fullback Alex Webster. And years later, after Sherman had been fired by the Giants, Webster replaced him. "My coaching philosophy is based on Jim Lee's," he acknowledged. "I want the best assistants I can find, and I want to give them total authority and all I will do is make final decisions and settle arguments. It's the only way I know."

Unfortunately, Webster didn't get the good staff he needed. Many of his assistants were "suggested" by team president Wellington Mara because they were "members of the family," so to speak. It was this sort of staff that doomed Webster, because his assistants were not qualified to handle authority on their own.

Lombardi did most of the coaching and the planning. So does Shula. Others, such as Ewbank and George Halas, allowed the staff personnel to get it together. But the quality of the athletes and the quality of the coaching staff dictated those moves. There is no magic ingredient.

In many cases, the reputations earned by assistant coaches from successful staffs parallel the reputations earned by superstar players from successful teams. For instance, Jethro Pugh was hailed as a new star at defensive tackle when he joined the Dallas Cowboys. And he played like it. But he had the advantage of playing next to one of the all-time great defensive tackles, Bob Lilly. And as Lilly aged, slowed, and needed less attention, Pugh's efficiency begin to decrease. Would Pugh have been an outstanding tackle on a mediocre team? Maybe not. But we will never know.

Not to downgrade Dallas, but another example of this found on the Cowboy's roster was middle line-backer Lee Roy Jordan, and this illustration can be tied to the presence, in the famed Giants' defenses, of Jordan's counterpart, Sam Huff. Both played for Landry, a defensive innovator. It was Landry's theory, developed early in the 1950s, that the middle linebacker is the quarterback of the defense and, as such, should be afforded the same protection from his lineman as the offensive quarterback is given by his.

Landry's middle linebackers needed quickness and agility. They did not have to be strong or physically dominant. They were shielded from blockers in order to maintain their freedom to roam, and defensive line play was designed to funnel the action into the middle, which not only prevented long and damaging sideline gains, but enabled the middle linebacker to make most of the tackles and, as a result, to be the focal point of the unit.

"Landry created Huff and Jordan," said former all-pro running back Frank Gifford. "I'm not saying they weren't sound players, but they sure weren't supermen. On other teams, with other coaches and other defensive philosophies, they might have had a lot of difficulty being stars . . . or starters. But they did what they had to do, what they were told to do, and it worked."

The myth, then, is that owners and general managers are basically competent. The reality would indicate otherwise. Trades, for instance, seem to backfire more often than not. Scores of waived players, cut loose by one team, have found employment, starting status, and even stardom on another team. Draft choices, especially first-round selections, are frequently disastrous. Why?

The most difficult assessment for the fan to make is on the subject of trades. So many peripheral factors are involved before the actual mechanics and motivations are known that the real issue is often left in shadows. Ideally, a trade is made to improve the team. In the case of a player-for-player trade, it should be a case of mutual satisfaction.

Two clichés:

"Sometimes, the best trades are the ones you don't make."

"A good trade is one that makes both teams happy."

Owners, general managers, and head coaches, reluctant to put themselves on the spot, generally prefer to make trades when they can deal off a draft choice for a player. They feel this places the onus of success on the other team a year later. It is this trading of draft picks, which is both too easy and too lightly treated, that is at the root of most of the weak teams' problems.

In a pure sense, the NFL should not allow the trading of high draft choices because, as originally conceived, the draft is structured to provide premium talent for the weak teams in order to ultimately achieve a balance of strength among the teams in the league.

To allow strong teams the luxury of stockpiling draft choices is to utterly destroy the draft theory, but the team that is frantic for help will grab at the offer of a proven veteran in return for such a gossamer factor as a future rookie. The team in need of immediate help will take the bait. The inherent blunder is that one or two proven veterans will not significantly improve that weak team. Only the patience of two or three fruitful years of drafting will alter the team as a whole.

Dallas, which is steered by shrewd and calculating men, has made a profit in recent years from the needs and blunders of weak teams. By conducting its own drafts with skill and foresight—not to mention buckets and barrels of incredibly good luck—the Cowboys long ago established a surplus of available player talent that builds upon itself.

General managers gaze at the Dallas roster with unbridled lust. "Most teams have about twenty good players on their rosters," said Jim Trimble, the pro personnel director of the Giants. "Teams like Dallas and Oakland and Los Angeles and Pittsburgh have thirty, maybe thirty-five. So when a team needs help immediately, that team has to go to those with the supply. But when you're in a spot, they know it, and you have to pay a fearful price."

Dallas readily admits to such a philosophy. "You use the tools given to you by the rules of the business," explained Gil Brandt, the co-architect, with General Manager and Vice President Tex Schramm, of this dynasty. "We don't like to trade away our high draft choices. But we would be less reluctant to trade away other teams' high picks, which we have acquired in trade for our surplus players. That way we can either acquire even higher picks or get the player we might really need. It's all a barter system, and when you can operate from a position of strength, you always have the upper hand."

In 1976, the only player not drafted by the Cowboys to make the forty-three-man roster was halfback Preston Pearson. He was signed as a free agent, and not at the price of having given up a player or a draft choice.

But some of the players traded away by the

Cowboys brought high and early draft choices, and those choices became Dallas starters and stars.

For example: In 1974, at midseason, the Giants discovered that they had to have another quarterback. At the same time in Dallas, Craig Morton was bitching that he was not given a chance to unseat the starter, Roger Staubach. And young Clint Longley was moaning that he should be "at least the second-string quarterback."

Morton, who had spent ten years with Dallas, had just about run out of value to the Cowboys. But to the Giants, he was salvation. The trade was made. The Cowboys acquired the Giants' first pick for 1975 and second pick for 1976. The Giants acquired Morton.

The Giants' first pick in 1975 was turned by Dallas into superman Randy White, now a starting defensive tackle out of Maryland. The second pick in 1976 was Jim Jensen, a fullback out of Iowa. In 1977, Jensen was traded—for another draft pick—to Denver. Morton was a flop in New York and was subsequently traded to Denver for Steve Ramsey, another quarterback. The Giants cut him in camp.

In May of 1977, the most eagerly sought college athlete available was Tony Dorsett, the Heisman Trophy-winning running back out of the University of Pittsburgh. Tampa Bay had the first draft choice but felt committed to the selection of running back Ricky Bell of Southern California. Seattle had the second choice. Dallas yearned for Dorsett. Seattle yearned for players, bodies, since it had just completed its first year of existence as an expansion team. Dorsett yearned to play almost anywhere but Seattle (he probably had similar nightmares about Buffalo, Green Bay, and Philadelphia, too).

It was a marriage made in Brandt-heaven. To Seattle

went the following draft choices: one first-round pick (fourteenth position), which the Cowboys had secured from San Diego in exchange for Longley (see how the loose ends get tied up?); three second-round picks (second position, acquired in a trade with Buffalo; thirteenth position, from a trade with San Diego; and twenty-sixth position, Dallas' own selection).

Finally, to compound the rape, Dallas reacquired its own second-round choice by sending to Seattle a wide receiver named Duke Fergerson, a man the Cowboys could not use. That reacquisition was turned into one of 1976's best available college quarterbacks, Glenn Carano of the University of Nevada-Las Vegas. What did Seattle get from Dallas? A guard from Tulsa named Steve August. A tackle from Boston College named Tom Lynch. A linebacker from Kansas named Terry Beeson. And Fergerson.

Dallas got Dorsett. On the street, Dallas might have got twelve-to-twenty for grand larceny and carnal abuse. In pro football, Dallas got a big hand. Seattle got a lot of snickers.

In 1974, the Cowboys chose defensive end Ed "Too Tall" Jones in the first round. He was the first player taken in the draft. But Dallas, which had only the twenty-second position, had made a trade with the Houston Oilers. The Cowboys had sent defensive end Tody Smith and wide receiver Billy Parks to the Oilers for Houston's first and third picks. Then the Oilers had the good grace to finish with the worst record in the league, and thereby earn the first draft choice. For Dallas. The third-round choice? Quarterback Danny White.

It has been this way in Dallas for years. In 1973 the second-round selection of wide receiver Golden Richards was made possible by an earlier trade with

Green Bay, in which the Packers received punter Rod Widby and cornerback Isaac Thomas. Also in 1973, the draft of subsequent all-pro defensive end Harvey Martin came about because of the use of a selection acquired from Houston for linebacker Tom Stincic. In 1972, the second-round choice turned up running back Robert Newhouse via a pick obtained from New England; the Patriots were given lineman Halvor Hagen and cornerback Honor Jackson.

Even in the first Dallas year, 1960, the Cowboys showed their intellectual superiority. Admitted into the league but given no part in the draft, Dallas countered by signing SMU quarterback Don Meredith to a "personal services" contract. Personal services? The NFL was in turmoil. "He works for us," said the Cowboys. "He might be clerking in our offices or an electrician at the stadium or a photographer. Hey, he might even wind up as a player, y'know?"

Since Meredith had not been drafted, the wise old Chicago Bears claimed him. Then they traded him—rather, they traded his rights—to Dallas. That made it "legal" for Dandy Don to play for the Cowboys. Two years later Dallas had to pay up—the Bears received a third-round draft choice.

Tody Smith . . . Billy Parks . . . Rod Widby . . . Isaac Thomas . . . Tom Stincic . . . Halvor Hagen . . .Honor Jackson. They were the commodities Dallas used to get the right to draft all-pro players. They hadn't amounted to very much while with Dallas, and they turned into veritable zeroes for their new teams. It should surprise no one.

The idealist's view that the results of a trade are equally beneficial to both teams is almost never realized. When it is, you can be sure that the two front office men most responsible for the deal were among the few truly qualified manipulators in the NFL.

The late Wells Twombly and I were trapped in Montreal during the 1976 Summer Olympics. The subject of trades and incompetence in front offices of pro sports franchises came up. It was Wells's conviction that we two, sitting in the University of Montreal dormitory where we were housed, could effect a trade.

"Take a loosely organized league, like the WHA. There must be two general managers who don't know each other. So we call, say, the Quebec Nordiques, and we tell them we are from the Peoria Pigs, or something, and we have to have their defenseman, Pierre La Puck. We are prepared to offer them our star center, Serge Le Sticke.

"Then we call Peoria and make the same offer in reverse. They both accept. So you tell the Peoria guy to make the announcement to his local press and, by the way, call the league office and make it official.

"The silly bastards will make the trade . . . and they'll both think they did a good thing."

We were going to do it. Unfortunately, Nadia Comaneci prevented an immediate offensive. But it would have worked. Absolutely. The only catch was to make it a vaguely reasonable trade.

Coaches and general managers—even owners—are sometimes as susceptible to the hero worship syndrome as the most devoted fan. The player with a collegiate reputation will be drafted high. Then, if he doesn't come right in and become Bronko Nagurski, the team that took him is embarrassed. And, more important, the team is ready to unload. Sometimes this is beneficial to another team. Sometimes it is fatal.

"Most kids out of college, with the exception of running backs, need time to learn all over again," said

John Ralston, who at the time was the head coach of the Denver Broncos. "You just cannot ask a young player with no NFL experience to walk in and start. When one does, it is almost always a surprise to the coaches. Even then, those exceptions are generally involved in playing the 'unskilled' positions."

Ralston was not downgrading rookie starters. The term "unskilled" position is a valid one in pro football. Such positions require the least amount of training, which is not to say no training at all. Just not as much. Defensive line positions are unskilled, since the primary factors necessary to perform there are the same as in junior high school—prodigious size, strength, quickness, and violent abandon. There is relatively little to "learn" about playing defensive tackle or defensive end. It is basically an instinctive assignment, with few additional lessons required.

"If they get into the backfield and drop the quarterback," said Merlin Olsen, the former all-pro defensive tackle of the Los Angeles Rams, "that's good enough. It almost doesn't matter how they do it, so long as it gets done." There are techniques that will make such a job easier, of course, and those will be learned and will thus refine a young defensive lineman. But the basics must be there. Power and strength and a wide streak of killer instinct. Presto!

Harder to accept but equally unskilled is the position of running back. "A runner is a runner when he gets out of college," said Jim Trimble. "You can't teach him how to be faster or how to slip away from a linebacker or how to make those instinctive cuts that he must make. If he can do them, he can do them. If he can't, he never will." The runner born with such abilities will be a pro runner. It really is as simple as that.

Neither John McKay at USC nor Lou Saban at Buffalo took O. J. Simpson and made him a running back. He was already a running back, and an incomparable one. The same can be said for Jim Brown, Gale Sayers, Walter Payton, and Larry Csonka. No coach taught them how to run. They refined techniques. The talent was there before player and coach ever met.

"For a while, Terry Metcalf was the most incredible running back I had ever seen," said Don Coryell, his coach at St. Louis. "The man had built-in radar, or heat sensors, or something equally improbable. He seemed to know where every possible tackler was on the field, whether he saw him or not, and we have films of Terry spinning away at the last second and leaving a linebacker grabbing air. He never saw the linebacker. He 'felt' him coming up. I wouldn't dare say I taught Terry how to do that, because even Terry doesn't know how he does it. It was something he had. We took advantage of it."

McKay, when he became head coach of the expansionist Tampa Bay Bucs, suffered through a winless fourteen-game schedule in 1976. This was the same man who, as coach at USC, was annually pushing his team toward national collegiate championships. After that first disastrous season, McKay, who had not lost his elfish sense of humor, neatly described his plight: "I keep a picture of O. J. on my wall," he said, "to remind me of what a great coach I used to be."

Most of the other positions, however, require time. Few rookies ever become outstanding quarterbacks overnight . . . or offensive linemen . . . or middle linebackers . . . or tight ends . . . or wide receivers. There is too much to learn, and much to unlearn.

The great Vince Lombardi released running back Timmy Brown, who went on to become one of the outstanding stars in the league in the 1960s. The great

Paul Brown released defensive tackle Henry Jordan, who became one of the cornerstones of the invincible Green Bay defense in the 1950s and 1960s. The great George Halas released fullback Bill Brown, who played a dozen seasons as the chief ground-gainer for the Minnesota Vikings. It happens every year. Rookies are released.

Rookies are claimed by other teams, mostly teams in need. Then the rookies develop into stars. Fortunately, it happens with all teams, so no single one of them stands out for the lion's share of embarrassment.

"There are some kids who need to go to two or three training camps before they learn the game," said John McVay, the head coach of the Giants. "Take an offensive lineman, a guard. That might be the most complicated position on the line, and at first look it's just overwhelming. They get buried in lessons, in technique. Some of them get cut and don't get picked up, so they try a year of minor league football. Then they wangle an invitation as a free agent tryout, and suddenly they can play."

Conrad Dobler of St. Louis, one of the NFL's top guards, went that route. So did guard Bob Keuchenberg of Miami. His partner at guard, Larry Little, was cut by San Diego. The man who played between them on all those Super Bowl teams, center Jim Langer, was cut by Cleveland.

In fact, it would be instructive to examine the Super Bowl dynasty established by Miami in 1972, 1973, and 1974, because head coach Don Shula did, in fact, build the team through other coaches' mistakes. Seldom if ever has one team made such capital on the errors of others. Kuechenberg was drafted by Philadelphia and cut as a rookie. He was claimed by Atlanta and cut. He then played for one year with the Chicago Owls of the old Continental League. He was signed as a free agent by Miami and went on to all-pro stature.

Little signed with San Diego as a free agent. He was undrafted and seldom played. Finally he was signed by Miami in a minor trade involving a defensive back named Mack Lamb (who, ironically, had been his teammate at Miami's Booker T. Washington High School). Little achieved five consecutive all-pro awards and twice was named the American Conference's Lineman of the Year.

Langer was signed as a free agent by Cleveland. He was released before the season ever started. Miami, desperate for centers, claimed him on waivers. He was a five-time all-pro center.

Tackle Norm Evans had been drafted in the fourteenth round by the Houston Oilers in 1965. He stayed in Houson for one season, and then was made available in Miami's expansion draft. Four times he was named to all-pro teams.

The other Super Bowl tackle, Wayne Moore, never even played college football. He was a basketball star at Lamar Tech and signed on with the San Francisco 49ers as a free agent tight end. He was tried there and at tackle and spent a season on San Francisco's reserve squad before being released and then claimed by Miami.

Thus the entire offensive line of the early 1970s, from tackle to tackle, came to Miami for almost nothing. Four of the five achieved all-pro status.

And what of the remainder of the team? It was, in many instances, a similar story.

Nick Buoniconti, the middle linebacker, was dealt off by the New England Patriots. He was too small for the position, only five eleven and 210 pounds.

Manny Fernandez, a defensive tackle, was signed as

a free agent by the Dolphins. He was a three-time all-pro. He had been undrafted largely because of a lack of height. He was only six one.

Maulty Moore, the other defensive tackle, had been signed as a free agent out of Bethune-Cookman College. Nobody wanted the six six, 265-pounder.

Doug Swift, the strongside linebacker, was signed as a free agent. He had played at Amherst College, one of the "sissy East Coast intellectual schools," which apparently negated his six three, 225-pound size and his 4.55 speed in the forty-yard dash. In fact, after being released by Montreal of the Canadian League, it was only Shula's friendship with Jim Ostendarp, the Amherst coach, that persuaded Don to give the kid a chance.

It was, then, a team with nine of its twenty-two starters, more than 40 percent, acquired through other teams' poor judgment. Those few with intelligence in this league have an absolutely unfair advantage.

Behind all of Shula's machinations and gyrations was Joe Robbie, the team's president. What he did best was leave Shula alone, having found contentment in the belief that he had the best man for the job. "I know about business," he said. "Don knows about football. We may not always agree [indeed, their relationship has often been stormy] but I don't dispute that which I don't know. I leave it to those who do know, and if they don't make things work, that's their problem."

Would that other owners thought like that. John Mecom in New Orleans, Gene Klein in San Diego, Ralph Wilson in Buffalo, Leonard Tose in Philadelphia, and Bud Adams in Houston, owners all, have continued to make news by spectacular interference. They have all gone through more than a reasonable number of head coaches and general managers, and it is sufficient to say that none of their teams has been involved in championship contention for years. Moreover, the prospect is bleak for such success in the near future.

One owner, however, has continued to win while interfering. He is Robert Irsay in Baltimore, a man who made his fortune in the air conditioning business in Chicago. He came into the league in unique fashion— he was persuaded to purchase the Los Angeles Rams and then "trade" franchises with Carroll Rosenbloom, who owned the Colts and wanted to push west. It was done. Irsay emerged as owner in Baltimore.

One of his first moves was to install Joe Thomas as general manager. Thomas had been in Minnesota and Miami as a team builder, and while his results were ultimately successful, his methods infuriated and alienated players, coaches, and, in some cases, owners. So Joe kept moving, leaving to others a legacy of winning.

Thomas tore up the rotting Colts' franchise and traded the old heroes, including quarterback Johnny Unitas. Others, such as John Mackey and Tom Matte, were convinced to seek retirement.

The first head coach hired was Howard Schnellenberger, who was fired on the field at halftime when Thomas and Irsay became enraged at a hapless performance. Then Ted Marchibroda was hired from the staff of George Allen in Washington. Marchibroda was quiet, competent, and as stubborn as Thomas. They had several flare-ups. In the summer of 1976. Irsay came into the locker room to berate the players for losing a game to Detroit—an exhibition game. Shortly after that, Marchibroda quit. Under pressure.

But the players backed him up. They demanded his

reinstatement. They threatened to retire from the team without his return. Irsay and Thomas relented, but the rift was irreconcilable. After the 1976 season, which ended with a first-round playoff loss to Pittsburgh, Thomas entered into new contract negotiations with Irsay. They were far apart, and Joe was intractable in his insistence on certain areas of authority.

Irsay countered his demands with predictable grace. He sent Thomas a letter delivered by his attorney, informing him that he had been dismissed. It was Christmas Day.

Marchibroda had won the war of nerves, but he was left to deal with Irsay on his own. It was, at best, a somewhat tainted victory.

Wellington Mara, who has been involved with the New York Giants for five decades, used to be one of the more successful "involved" owners. But his Giants last won a championship in 1963, and since then have had several seasons of record-setting incompetence. Finally, Wellington, whose nephew and son are now third-generation "Football Maras," stepped aside. He hired one-time all-pro defensive end Andy Robustelli as Director of Operations. Even that brought hoots from the detractors, since Robustelli, as most of the coaches and scouts before and after him, was a so-called family member, a former Giant. And Wellington didn't really step back, but just a bit to the side.

The man who once totally ran the team, made the trades, conducted the draft, and hired (and fired) the coaches, still exerts a powerful influence on team decisions. His early successes—acquiring for almost nothing such stars as Y. A. Tittle, Del Shofner, Alex Webster, and Erich Barnes—convinced him he could administer a team as well as anyone.

The bad trades apparently were forgotten. The hilarious draft choices were neatly obliterated. Only the continual lack of success on the field remained, a constant object lesson to other owners. They never learned, either.

11. Send This Boy to Camp

"Training camp is a terrible pain in the ass."
    —Alex Webster, as a player.

"The most important part of any team's season happens during training camp."
    —Alex Webster, as a head coach.

"I never bother to know the rookies, 'cause they ain't goin' to be around when the season starts anyhow."
    —Charley Conerly.

"We like to take as many free agents to camp as possible. All it costs is transportation, and we could find a player from out of all the mess."
    —Gil Brandt, Dallas Personnel Director

"You can't have too many people in camp, because it gets too disorganized and you can't give them all a fair chance."
    —Paul Brown, as a head coach.

If head coaches were denied the chance to see their veterans in camp. . . if all they had to look at were rookies for a month or so . . . they'd find twice as many young players as they do.
    —Obvious Truth

"When you're a rookie, training camp is fun. When you've been around for a few years, camp is a

necessary annoyance. When you start to get older,
it's a damned torture."
—Johnny Unitas, as a player.

Catch-22 thought: If a bad team practices at what
it does best, won't it just get worse?

The players are gathered. The draft is finished, the
chase for free agents has ended, and the veterans from
last year are assembled. It is time for the opening of
summer training camp.

This will be a late-summer/early-fall experience
spanning six to eight weeks, during which time the
NFL teams isolate and physically abuse their players
with twice-a-day workouts under a broiling sun, while
adding the further torment of mental anguish.

There are often more than one hundred warm
bodies in camp. There will only be forty-five when the
season starts, and in many cases the hopefuls have no
other careers to fall back on. They are football players.
They went to college to play football. They studied
football. They did not prepare for a career other than
football. "The player who gets straight-A grades,"
Alex Karras once said, only half-joking, "is a guy who
is letting his team down."

Joe Bailey is the business manager of the Dallas
Cowboys, but during summer camp Bailey becomes
travel agent, father confessor, and distributor of bad
news to the players who have been cut by the coaching
staff. "It's the worst part of my job," he says. "No
question about it. I see them right after coach Landry
tells them they're cut. The news usually hasn't sunk in
yet.

"They're still stunned and puzzled, wondering what
they're going to do next. A lot of these guys come from

small towns, and it's a really big deal in those places to have a guy in a professional camp. It's hard to go back and try to explain what happened.

"Plus, normal people go to college and major in something they can pursue when they get out. But these guys—for the most part—major in football. There is nothing else they can really do."

The Cowboys, notorious chart-makers and computer-users, ask the waived players to fill out a questionnaire. "Would you like to try again next year? What are your plans right now? Did you think you received a fair trial?"

There is another question: "Why do you think you were cut?" Bailey smiles. "One guy . . . we cut him right before the season opened . . . he wrote in 'I didn't have a chance to learn the plays properly.' Well, shit, he had been with us in camp for eleven weeks. That's a full college season, you know?" There are endless anecdotes about training camp.

The Giants, too, ask new players to fill out a personal history questionnaire:

Q: Do you play a musical instrument?
A: Yes.
Q: If so, which instrument?
A: Piano.
Q: How long?
A: About six feet.

"True, absolutely true," said the team's publicity director, Ed Croke. "That was one of the answers we got. And there have been lots of others like that. One kid, on the line that asked if he was married, said, 'No, but if it will help me make the team I'll find a girl and marry her.' Several of them have entered 'eating' when we ask for their hobbies."

There are sad stories in every summer camp. The Giants once cut a player in the morning. The night before, he had received a call from his wife telling him their house had burned down. He was without adequate insurance.

Another player received back-to-back jolts. The telephone on his dormitory floor rang (most teams rent college facilities for summer camp). It was for him. His father had died. No sooner did he hang up than one of the assistant coaches came up the stairs. "Coach wants to see you," he said, "and bring your playbook."

"Bring Your Playbook" . . . the saddest words of all to a pro football aspirant.

For sustained merriment, nothing can ever match the summer camp put in by a running back from Oklahoma named Joe Don Looney.

Joe Don had been the first-round draft choice of the New York Giants for the 1964 season. He was simply gorgeous, a six three, 225-pound blaster with uncanny inside power and deceptive outside speed. He had been twice an All-America at Oklahoma. All the scouting reports concurred. Looney was the proper choice, a sure-shot starter, soon to be a star.

There was just one thing wrong: Nobody scouted Joe Don's personality.

In the first two or three days, he had a run-in with Bill Wallace of *The New York Times*. It should be noted that in 1964, before the dramatic growth of the so-called "suburban area" newspapers, the single most important outlet as far as the Giants were concerned was the Great Gray Lady, *The Times*.

So Bill Wallace wandered up to Joe Don Looney's room one evening and knocked at the door. Joe Don answered. "Who are you?" he demanded.

"I'm Bill Wallace, and I'd like to interview you."

"Fuck you."

"But . . . but you can't say that. I work for *The New York Times*."

"Fuck *The New York Times*, too," said Joe Don Looney.

It had begun.

One day at practice, the rest of the team saw what it was the Giants had drafted. There was a tackling dummy built on a recoil steel spring to make it tougher to drive backward. The players were instructed to hit it and get the hell out of the way because it snapped back with tremendous force.

Well, Joe Don couldn't believe that. He was a physical fitness freak, building muscles on top of muscles, usually bare-chested to show what he had, and he refused to believe a machine could defeat him.

So he hit the thing and waited. Sure enough, it snapped back and knocked him on his ass. So he got up and hit it again. It hit him back again. On his ass. Joe Don began to yell at it and curse at it and it kept knocking him down. Finally he tore it off its mount and rolled around with it on the grass, kicking it and punching it and almost crying from frustration. It was more than a little frightening.

Finally, the droll Jimmy Patton turned to the man standing next to him. "Ah sure do hope," he drawled in Mississippian, "that somebody gets smart and doesn't give that old boy a knife and fork at dinner tonight."

It continued. His next act was to swear off practice. "I know the plays," he told head coach Allie Sherman, "so why the hell should I practice something I already know?"

Sherman, at wits' end, asked Y. A. Tittle, the elder statesman of the team and its star quarterback, to talk to Joe Don. Tittle agreed. He went to Looney's room and he stayed with the door shut for almost an hour. When he emerged, he looked baffled. "You know," he said, "I've been in this game for almost twenty years, and it never occurred to me. Why should we practice? I know the plays, too, by now." Then he giggled, shrugged his shoulders, and dismissed Joe Don Looney from his thoughts.

There was another Looney theory. It went "If I'm not tired at eleven o'clock, why should I have to go to bed and turn off my light and my radio?" Truly, there are no logical answers to these. It is simply curfew. Teams do it. Players abide by it.

"It's because we always do it that way," one of the assistant coaches explained.

"But I'm not tired yet," insisted Looney.

"Well, neither am I, but when I played I did it."

"Why?"

"Damned if I know. I just did it."

"Okay," said Joe Don. "I'll turn out my light and I'll shut off my radio. But I'll only pretend to sleep, okay?"

Joe Don Looney never made it to the opening game. The Giants traded him to Baltimore. Baltimore traded him to Detroit. From Detroit, he went to Washington. Then to New Orleans. Finally, he was out of football.

At last report, he was studying under a guru and living in a commune along the Ganges River in India. Gurus are short and fat, make millions of dollars by sticking their fingers in their ears and sticking their tongues out, and millions of misguided adolescents believe that is religion. Joe Don Looney understood that perfectly.

The Giants had another character in camp one year, a punter named Joe Whelan. After a while, Sherman cut him. A week later he spied Whelan in the dining room, eating with the players. He confronted him. "I was just waiting for you to catch me, coach. I didn't really have anything to do this summer until graduate school starts. This was great. Three meals a day . . . room and board . . . and after you cut me I didn't have to go to practice and get all sweaty, you know? Thanks for the vacation." Sherman couldn't understand that at all. But Joe Don Looney would have, had he still been around.

"Cutting players is the toughest thing in the world," said Alex Webster, when he was the Giants' head coach before he was cut by team president Wellington Mara.

"I'd tell a kid he just wasn't going to fit in and he'd start crying. One kid asked me to tell the press that he decided to leave and that I had begged him not to, because it would sound better back home. Another one got down on his knees and actually begged me for another chance. I gave it to him. The next week I had to cut him.

"Another kid got angry and said that he'd fight me, and if he won I'd have to change my mind. I kinda looked at him. Then I said, Listen, son, right now all you lost was a chance to play football. But you're workin' on losing a lot more, like your health.' He left."

Very often, the most dedication shown by players in summer camp is in getting out of summer camp. All teams impose a curfew, and all teams have that curfew broken with monotonous regularity. After all, young and healthy male animals will not be satisfied to dabble in football alone. There are any number who burn for the chance to have a late-night milkshake with a sister of the Salvation Army.

The Green Bay Packers of the 1960s, perhaps the closest any team has come to an established dynasty, also established themselves as one of the whackiest teams in NFL history. For openers, there was Paul Hornung and Max McGee. The Two Musketeers. The Lone Ranger and Tonto. The resident swingers. Stories are numerous and all true.

For instance, there was the time when Paul and Max were having great difficulty sneaking out of their dormitory. Vince Lombardi himself was conducting bed checks, and he knew all too well that the first room he'd better check was the one with the sign "Hornung-McGee" on the door.

One night the Terrible Twosome decided to make a point. As Lombardi walked down the hall, they made sure to slam the window down, slam a closet door, and engage in frantic (and loud) whispering. Lombardi was sure he had caught them coming in through the window. He burst into the room and spied them in bed. One bed. Convinced he'd find them still in street clothes, he tore off the covers. There they were—in a nude embrace. Lombardi, a Puritanical sort, blushed.

"Maybe we have been in camp a bit too long," he stammered,

Steve Wright and Bob Skoronski, two offensive tackles, were walking the campus of St. Norbert's college one evening. It was after the obligatory team meetings and before curfew (11 P.M.). They had walked a few blocks to a nearby ice cream parlor and were now walking back to the dorm with their cones. Wright finished his. Skoronski was still working on a chocolate chip dip when they spied Lombardi, a hundred yards away, approaching them. He, too, had taken a break for a short walk.

Skoronski panicked. He threw the remainder of his ice cream cone into a clump of bushes.

"Why the hell did you do that?" Wright asked.

"Listen, I know we're not doing anything wrong," Skoronski said. "I know we're not out late and I know there's nothing wrong with ice cream. But does he know it? How do I know how he feels about ice cream. Maybe he'll think I'm not concerned about my weight, or my condition. How the hell do you know what will turn him on? I ain't taking the chance." This was a six three, 250-pound man.

The work in training camp is exhausting, especially so for the reserves who understudy stars. Quite often, the older stars are saved for the games, allowed to go through training camp at their own pace. This is fine for the stars, impossible for the subs, for they have to work twice as hard taking the place of the veterans, yet never get to play in the games.

With the Philadelphia Eagles in 1946, the star running back was Steve Van Buren. He didn't practice. He was saved from that by head coach Greasy Neale, who wanted him ready to play when it counted. The reserve was a running back from Southern Cal named Mel Bleeker.

Day after day Bleeker would take Van Buren's place. Steve would jog along the sidelines, or sit on the bench, and poor Bleeker would run play after play. And because he wasn't a superstar, like Van Buren, Neale would scream at him for not making the play work as well as Van Buren handled it in a game.

Finally, after the second ninety-minute practice of the day, Neale called for the regulars to do extra work on a sweep he had installed. He called for almost all the regulars, that is. He told Bleeker to pretend he was Van Buren. And over and over they ran the sweep.

And over and over Neale would find fault with Bleeker's technique. "Bleeker, that's why you don't play . . . Bleeker, you can't trot, you have to run . . . Bleeker . . . Bleeker . . . Bleeker."

Bleeker rebelled. "Dammit, coach, I'm not Van Buren. I don't run the way he does. And I'm tired."

Neale responded. "Bleeker, if you don't run this next one hard you can just keep going."

They snapped the ball. It was tossed to Bleeker. He caught it, cradled it, and trotted to his left. And when he neared the sideline, he kept going. He turned and waved. " . . . so long, Greasy," he yelled. And he went into the locker room and changed and left the team. Neale tried to get him back. He refused.

"So long, Greasy" became the motto of the Eagles that season. They were 6-5, finishing second to the Giants' 7-3-1. Everyone wanted to think that Bleeker might have made the difference.

For most rookies, summer camp is traumatic. "I can remember my first year, my rookie summer," said quarterback Roman Gabriel. "There were the guys I had read about and watched on television and followed. And now I was one of them . . . the quarterback, which meant I had to give them orders and sometimes yell at them if they screwed up. It was too much. I just wasn't ready for that, so for a while I just didn't talk to anybody. I'd throw the ball downfield and then run after it and throw it back and run after it and like that. I just wanted to keep out of the way."

The lower draft choices and the free agents, especially those invited to the camp of a strong team, have almost no chance and they know it. The Jets once signed a free-agent quarterback named Harold Olsen. "Hell, I knew it was just until Joe Namath reported [he was conducting one of his famous summer camp holdouts]. I just hoped he'd get in before I was cut. The day he showed up, I was told to leave. But we had one practice together . . . it was my highlight."

Coaches start camp with, in many cases, well over one hundred players. More than half of them will have to be cut before the season starts. Those decisions, which affect dreams and hopes and incomes, are often made too quickly under pressure of having to get the squad down to league-mandated size, are prejudiced toward the veterans, who have already proven their abilities.

But the fringe veterans . . . the reserves who will never become starters . . . are just as paranoid as the free-agent and low-draft rookies. They know their status on the team, and they study each rookie who enters camp. "Sometimes, looking back on it now, the most exciting times of camp came on each cut-down day," said Charley Harper, a nondescript offensive lineman who stayed several years with the Giants. "Each week that passed and didn't claim me was a moral victory. I was a nervous wreck then, but now that I can look back at it, I guess it was kind of fun. Never knowing."

There is only one thing sadder than a one-time superstar who has finally lost his ability, and that is a one-time superstar who isn't aware of the loss.

"I knew it was time to retire," said wide receiver Raymond Berry, a Baltimore Colts' Hall of Fame member, "when I got a sprained neck one summer in camp. I had never had that happen, and when it did, I knew my body was telling me something."

But far too many former stars refuse to accept age. Sam Huff was traded by the Giants to the Redskins after head coach Allie Sherman sat him down and explained how Huff would have to play his middle linebacker position to compensate for a loss of speed. Huff refused to believe Sherman was right. Sherman traded him. It was enough of a jolt to make Sam see the light, and he got three more good years with the Redskins after deciding to play the way Sherman had explained in the first place.

"Worst thing I ever had to do," said Alex Webster, "was make Jim Katcavage my first cut as a head coach [1969]. He had been my teammate and my friend and now I had to cut him. We both did a little crying that day. But Kat just couldn't play anymore. It was sad to watch him try. He knew what to do, but his body just wasn't capable of doing it."

The rookies and the free agents live in a state of constant fear. The visit from "The Turk," the assistant coach or administrative aide who informs the player that "the coach wants to see you, and bring your playbook" is the most feared moment in camp.

"I remember having seven different roommates in eight weeks one summer," said Pete Gent, the Dallas wide receiver who turned into the author of *North Dallas Forty*. "Every time I'd get to remember whether it was Bill or Joe or Jack or Sam, he'd be gone and a new one would be in the bed next to me. Just my luck ... they were always guys."

Many rookies feel they have to "bulk up" before reporting to a training camp. Some, however, carry it to obscene lengths.

In 1966. the Giants drafted a defensive lineman named Don Davis from Los Angeles State. He was six six and 260. When he showed up the next July, he was six six and 330. He waddled. He jiggled. He couldn't play.

The late Les Bingaman, a notorious heavyweight, fooled the coaches. They never knew how much he weighed because the team (Detroit) didn't have a truck scale. One year some of the coaches wagered on Lester's poundage. The winner was the man who guessed 400. He was closest. Bingaman weighed 340.

Another intriguing part of summer camp is a team's desire to save the job of a fading veteran, a good friend. Y. A. Tittle remembers the summer when, as a San Francisco 49er, he led a movement to save linebacker Hardy Brown. "It was 1956," Tittle recalled, "and Hardy and I had been close friends for six, seven years. Well, he was on the verge of being dropped from the team. He wasn't the player he used to be, and he was in bad shape financially. He needed the job, and everybody knew he was about to lose it.

"Hardy was one of the team's most popular players, too, and we were having this big scrimmage on a Saturday, the kind that the coach (Frankie Albert) used just before he made final cuts. I knew if he had a good scrimmage, he'd stick around. So I told him I had an idea that might save his job.

" 'What is it?' he asked. I told him I invented a series of signals that would tip him off as to where the play was going. He kind of objected, but I told him it wouldn't really hurt anyone and he'd have a job. So he agreed.

"Well, when I got behind the center, I'd rub my hands together. If we'd run right, I'd lift up my right arm. Left . . . my left arm. If I didn't raise either one, we'd be going up the middle. And I'll be damned if Hardy didn't look like an all-pro all over again. He was filling holes when the run was there and he was knocking down passes, and every time I looked over at the sidelines Albert and his coaches were smiling,

"Then the coach did something I didn't expect. He took me out and sent in Earl Morrall, and Earl wasn't in on the plan. Hardy looked absolutely panic-stricken. But Albert also said he'd call plays for Earl, who was a young quarterback, and I managed to get word to Hardy to watch me on the sideline. Albert would say 'Dive Forty-Nine' and I'd put up my right arm and Hardy would know where to be. It worked great . . . and then Albert told the offense and defense to switch directions.

"Now he had to look back over his shoulder and he had reversed himself. When I raised my right arm, he went to his left. It didn't take long before he began to look silly. It got worse and worse, and every time they ran a play he was chasing the wrong way. It was embarrassing. When the scrimmage was over, they cut him."

So summer camp is a time when coaches cut, players worry, coaches suspect, and players sneak out.

"I wish there was a way to send my body to camp but not my head," said Larry Bowie, a former Minnesota guard. "If my head wasn't there, I wouldn't know how much it hurt."

But when camp is over, when the final roster is established, most of the hard work is behind the athletes. Coaches will work players nearly to death in summer camp—and the overzealous coaching staffs actually risk leaving their players' best performances in camp—but once the season begins they "save" the players for the games. It is true that though the summer camp period is impossibly difficult, the actual season, when everything counts, is much easier.

12. Other Myths to Puncture

"I used to read the Dallas playbook all the time. I just didn't like it. Everybody gets killed in the end."
—Pete Gent, Cowboy turned author.

The man was trying to convince Hank Stram, then Kansas City head coach, to draft Nebraska All-America Johnny Rodgers, a running back-turned-wide receiver. Stram demurred. "He's too much trouble," the coach allegedly said. "He's got a bad attitude. Hell, if we had him, I'd probably have to build him his own jailhouse."

The Rodgers-backer offered a small smile. "Then build it in the end zone, coach. Build it in the end zone. That's where he'll usually be."

"If I robbed a bank, I'd hide in the offensive line. Unless you jump offsides, nobody notices you there."
—Lou Holtz, former New York Jets' head coach.

"Most of the work we do is finished by the time the season starts. Summer camp is a bitch. The season is a piece of cake."
—Bob Tucker, tight end, Minnesota Vikings

"Placekickers aren't football players. They're hired feet. And they don't even know the rules."
—Alex Karras, former defensive tackle and all-pro.

"Placekickers don't bleed and they don't sweat, but when you kick a field goal to win the game with one second left, you make everything the players did worthwhile. If you miss the damned thing, nothing they did matters."

—Joe Danelo, Giants' placekicker.

On the average, a placekicker will get to try two field goals, two extra points, and five kickoffs in a game. Now multiply that by sixteen games, and he has a season total of thirty-two field goals, thirty-two extra points, and eighty kickoffs. That adds up to total playing time—with the clock running—of approximately fifteen minutes a season. The placekicker who earns $75,000 a year is making $5,000 a minute.

The only professional athlete's life less demanding than football is baseball, and neither the football player nor the baseball player could handle the intensity of a hockey, basketball, or soccer season.

For one thing, the football player who survives summer camp seldom, except for game day, engages in sustained physical activity during the season. There are, to be sure, practice sessions four or five days a week. There is one Game Day and one Off Day. But the day after a game is spent in light, limbering-up calisthenics or jogging, as is the day before the game. Furthermore, if the game is on the road, there is usually an even lighter and shorter warm-up drill before the team gets on the airplane and begins eating. Those players who stay in perfect condition during the season have done so on their own. Those who are in less than perfect shape far outnumber the others.

Coaches must operate under the premise that either

their players are in condition because they are athletes and have completed the rigors of summer camp, or that most of the players in the league are not really in top-notch condition.

A normal "heavy practice day" consists of an early morning reporting time for meetings with the coaching staff and film review. Then the players go out on the field for anywhere between one and two hours (it is a rare—and disliked—coach who will order full-equipment scrimmages during the week). There is almost no contact. The practices are planned and organized to get the most work done as far as preparing for the upcoming game.

This involves a great deal of skeleton passing drills—rushing the passer but not tackling him—conducted mainly for the benefit of the quarterback, his receivers and pass-coverage defenders, the line-backers, and deep backs. There are also some calisthenics . . . some tackling-dummy time . . . some jogging and sprinting . . . and then it's into the showers, after which there is either another meeting or a pat on the rump and the words: "Good job, Seymour. See you tomorrow."

Coaches justify this relative inactivity thusly: "You cannot overtrain or overwork the athletes, because they'll come up stale on Game Day. They are already in shape or they wouldn't be here. You don't want to leave your game on the practice field."

With all due respect, this is delightful bullshit. Vince Lombardi, for one, would have cackled himself silly at such nonsense. "The only real differences between a championship team and a raggedy-ass team is execution and stamina," he said. "You have to be sure they know their plays, and you want to know that when it gets into the fourth quarter, your guys won't break down and pant all over their shoes. Football is not a contact sport. It's an endurance test. Dancing is a contact sport. So is kissing."

Lombardi liked to point out that his teams in Green Bay, which were either champions or almost champions, always outscored the opposition in the final quarter. "You look at a team's statistics," he said, "and see how things are going in the fourth quarter. I'd bet that a team with less points than its opponents in the last period doesn't have a winning record. The team with more will have a winning record. It's one of the few statistics I pay any attention to at all, that and the number of plays a team had."

So, if all the hard work has been done in the summer, what is left to do during the season? Some coaches believe they must simply maintain the conditioning. They have far less control over their players once the season starts, too, for they are not living in a college dormitory, but out in the real world, arguing with their wives, taking out the garbage, mowing the lawn, eating and drinking according to their own desires, even staying up (horrors!) past 11 P.M.

"You have to treat them like men, which most of them are," said the late Don McCafferty, former head coach of the Colts and Lions. "Football is their income source. They won't fuck it up."

Which brings to mind Bobby Layne, the former Detroit and Pittsburgh quarterback, who in terms of carrying on, did so far longer and with far more élan than any other athlete in history.

There are too many Bobby Layne stories. Suffice it to say they all centered around his thirst and capacity for something stronger than ginger ale. "There were times he never even went to bed on a Saturday night," said one former teammate, speaking in a tone that can only be described as reverent. "He'd drive to the stadium from wherever he had been, take a shower, get into uniform and throw four touchdown passes. I don't think he had to sleep, and I'm not sure he'd know how to handle the fact of being totally sober."

(One of Layne's favorites had to be the late Joe E. Lewis, who once replied to a woman who said she never drank: "Do you mean to say that when you get up in the morning, that's as good as you're going to feel all day?")

They tell a story of Layne's days in Pittsburgh, where a young and foolishly brave halfback named Tom Tracy grew to idolize Layne, by then a seasoned (and well-preserved) veteran. Week after week, Tracy would plead with Layne to take him along on a Saturday night foray. Week after week, Layne would rebuff the eager Tracy. But his entreaties were too much, and finally Layne agreed. It was a Saturday night before a home game, and the odd couple hit every watering hole in western Pennsylvania. That was routine for the quarterback, but a new world for the halfback.

Then came the game. Layne was bouncy and bright, never needing sleep. Tracy was totally miserable. And Layne called a deep pass play. It was Tracy's number. Down the field he raced, staggering each foot in front of the other. The ball was perfectly thrown, but Tracy couldn't get to it. He trudged back upfield, head pounding. In the huddle, Layne called the very same play.

"My God, Bobby, have a heart," gasped Tracy. "You know where I was last night."

Layne regarded him with a cold stare. "If you can't serve the time, don't do the crime," he snapped. Tracy was cured. Motivated by only the most noble instincts for self-preservation, he never forayed with Layne again.

That is how some players maintain top condition once released from prison (summer) camp.

Another of the myths, and one apparently too seductive to be rejected by most general managers and head coaches, is that a good player on a good team will be a good player on a lousy team.

Instead, let's do it this way. If Lee Roy Jordan did not play for the Dallas Cowboys, where he earned almost annual all-pro honors as a middle linebacker, would he have done the same elsewhere?

"No, I'm sure he wouldn't have been nearly as effective anywhere else," said Frank Gifford. "Lee Roy was a fine athlete. I'm not downing him. But he played for the one man [Tom Landry] who treats his middle linebackers differently. Tom protects them, as an offense protects its quarterback. So he has freedom to roam and freelance. And Tom's defense is designed to act like a funnel, forcing everything inside, up the middle, where the middle linebacker can strike the final blow and get a lot of tackles.

"When Tom was the defensive coach in New York, he did the same thing for Sam Huff. Lee Roy Jordan was Tom's new Sam Huff. Both of them were fine athletes, but I don't think either of them were great middle linebackers, not like Schmidt or Nitschke or Butkus."

But how many times—hundreds? thousands?—has a trade been made which brought to a weak team a member of a strong team? And how much hope was blown away thereafter? And how much time had been wasted when the team should have been drafting and growing its own stars, tailored to fit its scheme?

The Giants of the 1950s and early 1960s serve as one example. The defensive front four was composed of ends Andy Robustelli and Jim Katcavage, tackles Rosey Grier and Dick Modzelewski. All were marvelous athletes. Robustelli was great. Grier was great when he chose to be. Modzelewski was a notch or two below them. Katcavage was the weak link, but that is no more than a relative evaluation. And this becomes clear when it can be said that an offense faced with this defensive line invariably chose to attack Katcavage's end. Being on a line like this served to make Katcavage more dangerous, more effective; in fact, a better player.

But then Robustelli retired. And Grier was traded. And Modzelewski was traded. And suddenly Katcavage, still young, was accompanied by three other linemen whose best days would not have equaled a good practice-while-injured day for the three who had departed.

Did Katcavage improve this new line? To a degree, because it would have been even worse without him. But just as his presence made possible some improvement, it hurt the Robustelli-Grier-Modzelewski line simply because he wasn't as good as those three. Katcavage needed a great line to play well.

Dallas has never traded anyone who has gone on to stardom. (In summer camp of 1975, they did cut a quarterback named Jim Zorn, who went on to lukewarm stardom with the expansion Seattle Seahawks, but he was a free-agent rookie and could not have made the squad in Dallas—that year—under any circumstances.)

Neither has Oakland nor, in recent years, Pittsburgh, ever traded anyone who has gone on to make them regret the move. Miami culls have never worked out, either. None of the old Packers were sent out to become stars elsewhere, though, Lord knows, teams tried to borrow the magic in the persons of Lee Roy Caffey, Tommy Crutcher, Steve Wright, Earl Gros, Al Jacobs, and Travis Williams. In short, a great team is peopled by great athletes. But a team without many great athletes will pull down those who are, with perhaps a few exceptions.

There is a more basic question involved, and it concerns the running backs and quarterbacks, the glamour boys of the profession. Is a runner great because of his talent or his offensive line? Is a quarterback great because of his passing ability or his protection? Can a "great" runner maintain his greatness on a team with a tissue-paper line? Will a great quarterback continue to throw touchdown passes and win games playing behind an inept blocking wall?

The answer, generally, is this: A great runner will make a poor line a bit better, but he'll kill himself in the doing. And a great quarterback will find it more difficult to find his tertiary receiver or read a complicated defense when he is lying flat on his back, ribs throbbing and staring at two skies.

There have been, of course, impossibly bad teams with one great player. Pittsburgh with John Henry Johnson; Buffalo with O. J. Simpson; Chicago with Gale Sayers; Chicago with Dick Butkus. The player was great, the team was lousy, its record reflected its overall deficiencies, and the shame of such a situation is that superstars such as Johnson, Simpson, Sayers, and Butkus, never had much of a chance to get into championship games.

In the case of the Cleveland Browns, the addition of fullback Jim Brown caused the coaching staff to acquire a top offensive line so as to enhance his abilities. As a result, players such as Gene Hickerson, Dick

Schafrath, and John Wooten were brought in, but Brown spent as much time coaching them as did the coach paid to work with the offensive line.

All this improvement caused the Browns to do that which they were unprepared to do—they made it to NFL championship games in 1964 and 1965. But the rest of Brown's career was spent with Cleveland chasing New York, Dallas, and Philadelphia. The greatest fullback in pro football history—yes, that includes Marion Motley, Jim Taylor, Larry Csonka, and Bronko Nagurski—played in just three championship games. And the greatest halfback in pro football history, O. J. Simpson, saw exactly one first-round playoff game (a 32-14 loss to Pittsburgh) in all his storied years with the Buffalo Bills.

One shudders to imagine Simpson behind such modern lines as Los Angeles, New England, Oakland, or Dallas. Legislation by the federal government might have been the only way to keep him under twenty-five hundred yards a season.

Paul Wiggin, former head coach of the Kansas City Chiefs, was talking about one of his team's several losses during the 1977 season. What marked this one as any different from all the rest, in his mind, was the ease with which the New England Patriots had blitzed Wiggin's offense and dropped his quarterback, Mike Livingston. "It was an all-or-nothing defense," Wiggin said, trying a wry and wan smile. "They got it all, we got nothing."

Wiggin was particularly distraught over a few nine-man stampedes, which red-dogged the three Patriot down linemen, the four linebackers, and one each cornerback and safety. "It shouldn't have been a problem," he said. "We had just as many people on the field as they did. The big secret is to match up with their people, one for one."

In the 1977 season, Atlanta's defense had done the same thing to the Giants' offense. That resulted in nine sacks of the quarterback and seven Giant holding penalties by the embattled offensive linemen.

John McVay, the Giants' head coach, offered the same philosophy as Wiggin's. "Hell, there's just no excuse for not being able to stop a heavy rush," he said. "If they send nine guys, you put nine guys in front of them. If they send only four or five, you get extra men to play with. We have blocked out those kind of defenses before, but sometimes players forget."

Both Wiggin and McVay were vindicating an age-old offensive theory, put forth in the early days of football when Ivy League colleges ruled the nation, and the forward pass was a heretical thought. "If you put your guys where their guys are," it was said, "then their guys won't be able to hurt you. And if one of them makes a mistake, you have a touchdown."

Students nodded sagely. On their way home, they would slow their horses to a casual canter and repeat the litany " . . . put your guys where their guys are . . . I see! It's brilliant!" So how come the pro football teams forget?

Because nobody bothers with basics and fundamentals anymore, that's why. Because they are so involved in the mumbo-jumbo of secret languages and mysterious terminology they forget the basic tenets of the game. With eleven men on each side, you should be able to do no worse than achieve a stalemate.

Here's another myth: There is really very little difference between any of the NFL teams. There isn't much to separate a team with a 4-10 record from one with a 10-4 record.

All of you who believe that please line up on the right side of the room. The Easter Bunny and the Tooth Fairy will be right over to take your holiday orders.

"There are five or six top teams," said Tom Myers, a safety for the New Orleans Saints. "Then there are the bulk of the teams, maybe eighteen or twenty. Then there are four or five absolute stiffs. Those are the teams you know you can beat, and you pray for the schedule to put you together [with them]. Besides, for each stiff you get, that's one less chance to play one of the great teams and get your butts kicked."

And so, dear reader, we have hit on another truth. The players on the "stiff" teams simply cannot perform to the same level as their counterparts on the top teams. And if a top team gets out on the field with a stiff, the top team can play at 75 percent efficiency and beat the stiff team playing at 100 percent efficiency.

One of the most cherished clichés in the NFL is this: "On any given Sunday, any NFL team can beat any other NFL team." Dear Lord, what a crock!

In 1976, the Tampa Bay Buccaneers got the chance to play the Oakland Raiders. The score was 49-16. Tampa Bay had the 16, and went on to compile a perfect 0-14 record. Oakland had the 49, and went on to compile an almost-perfect record . . . 13-1 during the season, 16-1 overall, and culminating this with a perfectly effortless Super Bowl XI victory over Minnesota.

Tampa Bay could have played Oakland every Sunday that year and not won a game. The only possible chance that existed was that, since the Bucs were younger than the Raiders, old age would have claimed the Oakland athletes first.

But it is not fair to put all of this on Tampa Bay. There were, in 1977, any number of teams that could have continued to play Oakland—or Pittsburgh, or Baltimore, or New England, or Cincinnati, or Dallas, or Minnesota—with no chance of winning. It is simply that Tampa Bay had become a standard of (negative) perfection, which makes it easy to use as a measuring device.

Contrary to what you may have heard, not all pro football players move their lips when they read or correspond with loved ones by using crayons and construction paper. Some of them are downright intelligent, and at least that suffering minority knows very well what sort of season is in store.

"What we are really hoping for this season," said one such poet laureate, "is that we don't lose more games than we win. But I don't think there's much chance of that. We were mathematically eliminated from our division championship the second they released this year's schedule. We just can't compete."

Very often, not being able to accept either defeat or the reality of responsibility, such players will make demands—usually through the press—that they be traded. "We just aren't making any progress," they claim, "and I'd like something to show for my years in the league." What they always fail to realize is that they do, indeed, have something to show for their efforts—a long and unbroken series of salary checks which, if totaled, would add up to four score and seven times more than they might have made pumping gas or serving up tall ones to the local sots.

The trouble with teams that "make no progress" is usually the caliber of the players, including those who want to be traded to the good teams. There is, of course, no valid reason, in nine-out-of-ten instances, to think that the good teams want them. But fooling oneself is another time-honored amusement among professional athletes.

It goes hand-in-hand—or is that tongue-in-cheek?—with the Pro Football Mystique.

ABOUT THE AUTHOR

DAVE KLEIN writes a sports column for the Newark *Star-Ledger* and the Newhouse Newspapers. He has covered the New York Giants since 1961 and has written for many national sports publications. His newspaper stories have frequently appeared in *Best Sport Stories of the Year*, and in 1974 he won the best-in-book award for his coverage of the Bobby Riggs-Billie Jean King tennis match. His previous book, *The Game of Their Lives*, the story of the participants in the 1958 sudden-death playoff between the Baltimore Colts and the New York Giants, was highly praised, and is available in a Signet paperback edition. Mr. Klein lives in Scotch Plains, New Jersey, with his wife, Carole, and their children, Aaron and Mindy.

SIGNET Sports Books You'll Want to Read

☐ **PLAYING PRO FOOTBALL TO WIN by John Unitas with Harold Rosenthal.** Revised and updated. A bruising inside look at the pro game by the greatest quarterback of them all. With 16 pages of exciting photos!
(#W7209—$1.50)

☐ **THE COMPLETE HANDBOOK OF PRO FOOTBALL, 1978 EDITION edited by Zander Hollander.** Now you can get 28 NFL team yearbooks in 1 in the most comprehensive handbook available from First Kickoff to Super Sunday. The one guide you'll need for the '78 season includes 28 NFL scouting reports, rosters, official stats, Monday night TV, schedules, plays, draft, and much more.
(#E8233—$2.25)

☐ **THE COMPLETE HANDBOOK OF COLLEGE FOOTBALL, 1978 EDITION edited by Zander Hollander.** Here is the one guide to have for college football from the first coin toss to the Rose Bowl! Includes 300 team previews, college All-Americans, top 20 picks, TV games, schedules, stats, and much more. (#E8234—$2.25)

☐ **PAPER LION by George Plimpton.** When a first-string writer suits-up to take his lumps as a last-string quarterback for the Detroit Lions, the result is "the best book ever about pro football!"—Red Smith. "A great book that makes football absolutely fascinating to fan and non-fan alike . . ."—The New York Times
(#J7668—$1.95)

☐ **THE BEST TEAM MONEY COULD BUY: The Turmoil and Triumph of the 1977 New York Yankees by Steve Jacobson.** Baseball has entered a new era of millionaire ballplayers and sensitive psyches. This is the very candid inside story of the team that made winning baseball a whole new ballgame. (#J8002—$1.95)

☐ **MY LUKE AND I by Eleanor Gehrig and Joseph Durso.** The poignant love story of Lou and Eleanor Gehrig—the glory and tragedy she shared with the "Iron Man of Baseball." With 16 pages of rare, personal photos.
(#E7818—$1.75)

Other SIGNET Books of Special Interest

☐ **WHERE HAVE YOU GONE JOE DI MAGGIO? The Story of America's Last Hero by Maury Allen.** In the words of those who knew all the different parts of him, Joe Di-Maggio, his fascinating era, his unforgettable exploits, his personal agonies, his meaning then and now, brought together in a portrait to read and to treasure. "Magnificent . . . like **The Boys of Summer**, this book will fascinate!"—The Atlantic (#W6986—$1.50)

☐ **THE BOYS OF SUMMER by Roger Kahn.** This bestseller of the Brooklyn Dodgers then and now recaptures "memories so keen that those of us old enough can weep, and those who are young can marvel at a world where baseball teams were the center of a love beyond the reach of intellect, and where baseball players were worshipped or hated with a fervor that made bubbles in our blood."—Heywood Hale Broun, Chicago Tribune (#J8493—$1.95)

☐ **SPORT MAGAZINE'S ALL-TIME ALL STARS edited by Tom Murray.** The top 22 players in major league baseball history—the way they really were. This is a book about the way each of them played the game. The way each of them lived his life. The way it is and what it takes to be the very best. (#J7650—$1.95)

☐ **HOLISTIC RUNNING: Beyond the Threshold of Fitness by Joel Henning.** With an Introduction from the National Jogging Association. From blisters to bliss—the first total guide to the exercise and ecstasy of running. (#E8257—$1.75)*

☐ **HOW TO SUCCEED IN TENNIS WITHOUT REALLY TRYING by Shepherd Mead.** From shotmaking to sex—everything your pro will never teach you (and your opponents don't want you to know!) . . . "Enlightened . . . informed . . . very rewarding!"—Arthur Ashe (#E8020—$1.75)

☐ **THE PERFECT JUMP by Dick Schaap.** What happens to a world-record-breaking athlete when he's reached that once-in-a-lifetime perfection he can never achieve again? The glory and heartbreak of an athlete who reached the top and had nowhere left to go. With an exciting sports photo insert! (#E7248—$1.75)

*Price slightly higher in Canada

Big Bestsellers from SIGNET

☐ **SONG OF SOLOMON by Toni Morrison.**
(#E8340—$2.50)*

☐ **RAPTURE'S MISTRESS by Gimone Hall.**
(#E8422—$2.25)*

☐ **PRESIDENTIAL EMERGENCY by Walter Stovall.**
(#E8371—$2.25)*

☐ **GIFTS OF LOVE by Charlotte Vale Allen.**
(#J8388—$1.95)*

☐ **BELLADONNA by Erica Lindley.** (#J8387—$1.95)*

☐ **THE GODFATHER by Mario Puzo.** (#E8508—$2.50)*

☐ **KRAMER VERSUS KRAMER by Avery Corman.**
(#E8282—$2.50)

☐ **VISION OF THE EAGLE by Kay McDonald.**
(#J8284—$1.95)*

☐ **HOMICIDE ZONE FOUR by Nick Christian.**
(#J8285—$1.95)*

☐ **CLEARED FOR THE APPROACH by F. Lee Bailey with John Greenya.** (#E8286—$2.50)*

☐ **CRESSIDA by Clare Darcy.** (#E8287—$1.75)*

☐ **DANIEL MARTIN by John Fowles.** (#E8249—$2.95)

☐ **THE EBONY TOWER by John Fowles.** (#E8254—$2.50)

☐ **THE FRENCH LIEUTENANT'S WOMAN by John Fowles.**
(#E8535—$2.50)

☐ **RIDE THE BLUE RIBAND by Rosalind Laker.**
(#J8252—$1.95)*

☐ **MISTRESS OF OAKHURST—Book II by Walter Reed Johnson.** (#J8253—$1.95)

☐ **OAKHURST—Book I by Walter Reed Johnson.**
(#J7874—$1.95)

☐ **THE SILVER FALCON by Evelyn Anthony.**
(#E8211—$2.25)

☐ **I, JUDAS by Taylor Caldwell and Jess Stearn.**
(#E8212—$2.50)

☐ **THE RAGING WINDS OF HEAVEN by June Shiplett.**
(#J8213—$1.95)*

*Price slightly higher in Canada